Current Chinese Economic Report Series

The Current Chinese Economic Reports series provides insights into the economic development of one of the largest and fastest growing economies in the world; though widely discussed internationally, many facets of its current development remain unknown to the English speaking world. All reports contain new data, which was previously unknown or unavailable outside of China. The series covers regional development, industry reports, as well as special topics like environmental or demographical issues.

More information about this series at https://link.springer.com/bookseries/11028

Zhongguancun Listed Companies Association

The Growth Report of Zhongguancun NEEQ Listed Companies (2021)

Springer

Zhongguancun Listed Companies
Association
Zhongguancun Listed Companies
Association
Beijing, China

ISSN 2194-7937 ISSN 2194-7945 (electronic)
Current Chinese Economic Report Series
ISBN 978-981-19-1241-2 ISBN 978-981-19-1242-9 (eBook)
https://doi.org/10.1007/978-981-19-1242-9

This Springer imprint is published by the registered company Springer Nature Singapore Pte Ltd.
The registered company address is: 152 Beach Road, #21-01/04 Gateway East, Singapore 189721, Singapore

Editorial Board of *The Growth Report of Zhongguancun NEEQ Listed Companies (2021)*

Contents

About the Author

Zhongguancun Listed Companies Association (ZLCA) founded autonomously by a number of listed companies in Zhongguancun is a national NGO registered under the Bureau of Civil Affairs of Beijing. The association was officially established on August 16, 2012.

ZLCA's mission is to assist government in delivering and implementing policies, representing members in providing advices and suggestions to government, providing professional policy consultation for its members, and establishing a high-level networking, resource sharing, and learning platform.

The foundation of ZLCA will play an important role in helping listed companies operate normatively and develop healthily, building a bridge between listed companies, investors, capital market supervisory bodies and government, and promoting sharing of resources and cooperation.

Objectives

- **Observation of Authoritative Data**
  Through the analysis of growth data, the study of growth pattern and the publication of the annual competitiveness report of ZLCA. This association aims to assist the government, members, and investors in their relevant project research and development strategies for member companies.
- **Communication Bridge**
  We are committed in the communication between listed companies, investors, market regulators, and government in order to improve their mutual understanding by respecting needs and views.
- **Promotion for Innovation**
  We strive to facilitate the development of initiative companies. We also wish to support companies listed on Growth Companies Market and promote technological innovation in Zhongguancun.

- **International Influence**
  We will host international conferences and activities and organize overseas roadshows with group visits to boost the international influence of companies in Zhongguancun.

Chapter 1
The Development Characteristics and Sugestiones of the Zhongguancun NEEQ in 2020

1.1 The Development Characteristic of Zhongguancun NEEQ Market in 2020

1.1.1 The Number of NEEQ Delisting Companies Has Declined for the First Time and the Reform Comes into Force

1.1.1.1 The Number of Listed Companies

As of December 31st, 2020, the number of Zhongguancun NEEQ Listed Companies was 1073. This report excludes the companies that have been delisted[1] and have not been published[2] in the annual reports, only taking the 912 companies as the research objects[3] that publicly announced their 2020 annual reports before April 30st, 2021.

The number of Zhongguancun NEEQ Listed Companies has declined for four consecutive years. In 2020, the number of these companies was 912, which was a 36.93% decrease from the highest point in 2017; the number of listed companies decreased by 169, which was higher than the number of 143 companies in the same period last year. In terms of the number of newly listed companies, there will be 7 new companies, whcich increased in single digits for the first time (Fig. 1.1).

---

[1] The delisting company here refers to the Zhongguancun NEEQ company that was delisted from January 2020 to December 31st, 2020.

[2] It refers to the Zhongguancun NEEQ company that has not disclosed the 2020 annual report before April 30st, 2021.

[3] The research objects in this book are Zhongguancun NEEQ listed companies, that is, companies whose industrial and commercial registration is in Beijing and are listed on the NEEQ system, excluding companies listed on the two networks (STAQ and NET) and delisting company from the main board.

Zhongguancun Listed Companies Association, *The Growth Report of Zhongguancun NEEQ Listed Companies (2021)*, Current Chinese Economic Report Series,
https://doi.org/10.1007/978-981-19-1242-9_1

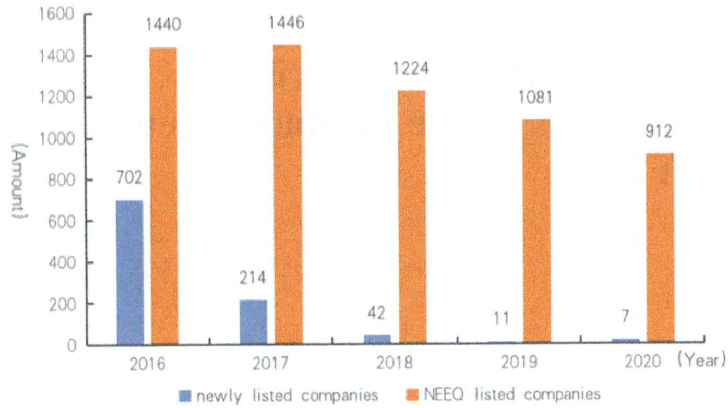

Fig. 1.1 The number of Zhongguancun NEEQ listed companies and newly listed companies in 2016–2020 (*Source* Wind, compiled by ZLCA)

From the angle of market classification, the number of Zhongguancun NEEQ innovation companies has increased substantially in 2020. As of the end of 2020, among the Zhongguancun NEEQ Listed Companies, there are 7 select companies (Table 1.1), accounting for 0.77% of the number of these companies, and 17.07% of the number of all select companies in the country, which ranks first in China; the number of Zhongguancun NEEQ innovation companies is 136, accounting for 14.91% of the Zhongguancun NEEQ Listed Companies, an increase of 46 from the 90 in 2019, a year-on-year increase of 51.11% (Table 1.2).

1.1.1.2 The Number of Delisting Companies

In 2020, in line with the trend of national NEEQ delisting companies, the delisting companies of NEEQ in Zhongguancun will decline for the first time. In 2020, a total of 903 NEEQ companies across the country were delisted, and this number decreased by 54.55% compared with 2019. Among them, a total of 115 Zhongguancun NEEQ companies chose to delist, and the number decreased by 55.42% compared with 2019. The decline in the number of delisting companies was slightly lower than that of the whole country (Fig. 1.2).

A detailed analysis of the reasons for the delisting of Zhongguancun NEEQ listed companies in 2020. Among them, 62 companies were delisted due to production and operation adjustments, accounting for 53.91%; the number of companies delisting due to other non-compliance with the listing situation was 25, accounting for 21.74%; companies that did not disclose regular reports after the suspension of listing are 22, accounting for 19.13%; 6 companies have been delisted due to the backdoor listing, accounting for 5.22% (Fig. 1.3). As of April 30st, 2021, a total of 31 Zhongguancun NEEQ companies have successfully transferred to Shanghai and Shenzhen A shares. Among them, of the 6 companies that were delisted due to the transfer of board

Table 1.1 List of Zhongguancun NEEQ select companies in 2020

Rank	Stock code	Name	Launch date	Company attribute	Market Classification	Wind Industry
1	430047.NQ	NORTHLAND	2020-11-24	private enterprises	Select	Manufacturing
2	832317.NQ	SKYCAM	2020-07-27	private enterprises	Select	Scientific research and technology service
3	833819.NQ	NUTRICHEM	2020-07-27	private enterprises	Select	Manufacturing
4	834021.NQ	GOLDEN TIMES	2020-07-27	private enterprises	select	Information transmission, Software and IT services
5	835184.NQ	GRAND TECH	2020-07-27	private enterprises	select	Information transmission, Software and IT services
6	835508.NQ	IN-TO	2020-07-27	private enterprises	select	Information transmission, Software and IT services
7	836263.NQ	ZHTD	2020-07-27	private enterprises	select	Management of Water Conservancy, Environment and Public Facilities

Source Wind, compiled by ZLCA

Table 1.2 The classification of Zhongguancun NEEQ listed companies in 2019–2020 (Unit: Number, %)

Year	Classification	Select		Innovation		Base	
	Amount	Amount	Ratio	Amount	Ratio	Amount	Ratio
2019	1081	–	–	90	8.33	991	91.67
2020	912	7	0.77	137	15.02	768	84.21

Source Wind, compiled by ZLCA

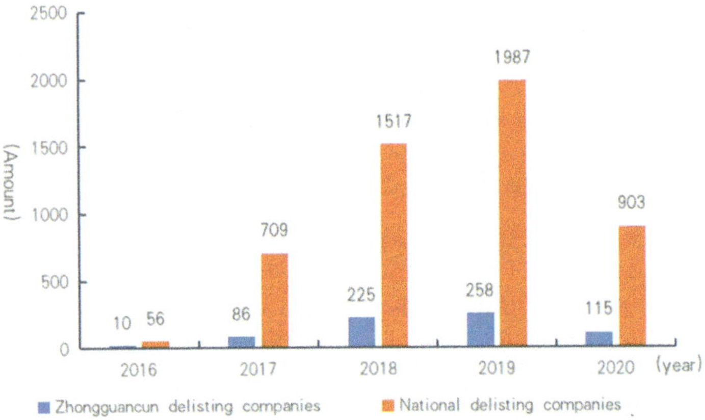

Fig. 1.2 The number of delisting companies on the national and Zhongguancun NEEQ in 2016–2020 (*Source* Wind, compiled by ZLCA)

Fig. 1.3 The reasons for delisting of Zhongguancun NEEQ delisting companies in 2020 (*Source* Wind, compiled by ZLCA)

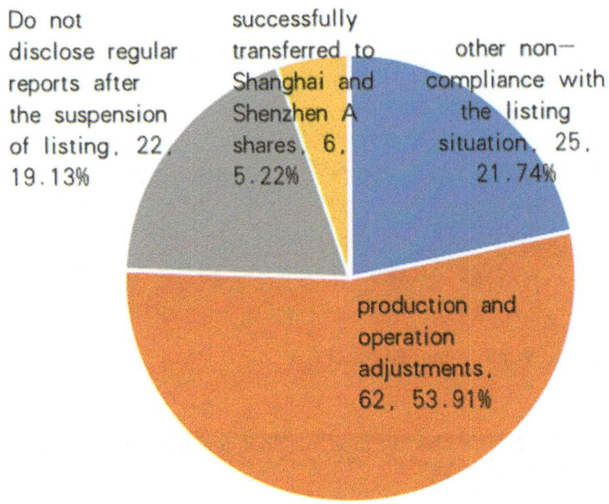

in 2020, 5[4] have successfully listed on the Shanghai and Shenzhen A-shares (2 successfully listed on the STAR Market and 3 on the ChiNext Board) (Table 1.3).

In general, the number of Zhongguancun NEEQ delisting companies declined for the first time, which was the lowest in the past three years. From the perspective of the structure of the reasons for delisting, the proportion of companies that actively delisted due to production and operation adjustments and backdoor listing has exceeded half of the total delisting for the first time. Among them, the proportion of delisting due to production and operation adjustments will increase from 34.88% in 2019 to 53.91% in 2020; the proportion of delisting due to the backdoor listing has also increased from 3.49 to 5.22%. In contrast, the proportion of passively delisting companies is getting smaller and smaller. There are two main reasons for this phenomenon:

First, the reshuffle of the Zhongguancun NEEQ market and the market-oriented exit mechanism have produced an exit ecology of survival of the fittest. The NEEQ market implements a market-oriented exit mechanism. On the one hand, it respects the independent willingness of enterprises to delist, and on the other hand, it also insists on clearing out inferior enterprises. Since the National Equities Exchange and Quotations System (hereinafter referred to as "NEEQ") implemented in 2006 mandatory delisting of two listed companies that failed to disclose their 2015 annual reports on time for the first time, the NEEQ released the "Detailed Rules for the Delisting of Listed Companies (Draft for Comment)" in October, 2016 and the "Guidelines for the Application and Withdraw for Delisting of Listed Companies on the NEEQ" in March, 2019. The new "Implementation Rules for the Delisting of Listed Companies on the NEEQ" optimizes the procedures and conditions for active delisting, and adds four categories of twelve types of mandatory delisting, demonstrating the market's determination to clear out inferior companies. From the delisting data in recent years, it can also be seen that from 2017 to 2020, the total number of Zhongguancun NEEQ delisting companies was 684, accounting for 47.30% of the highest point of 1,446[5] Zhongguancun NEEQ companies. It can be said that the market-oriented exit mechanism has achieved remarkable results

[4] SINOHYTEC (688339.SH) focuses on the R&D and industrialization of hydrogen fuel cell engine systems; BEIJING JIAODA SIGNAL TECHNOLOGY (300851.SZ) mainly focuses on the R&D, organization of production, sales and technical support of key equipment of the control system of rail transit trains, such as transponder systems, locomotive signal on-board equipment and track circuit readers. The products developed by it have achieved the highest safety integrity level SIL4 in the industry;CDS (300846.SZ) is an Internet data center service provider, which covers the whole world and is dedicated to providing global cloud-network integrated solutions for Chinese companies going overseas; IAT (300825.SZ) mainly provides vehicle-related services for fuel vehicles and new energy vehicles; INHAND (688080.SH) is a provider for industrial Internet of Things communication products and "cloud + terminal" overall solutions in the Internet of Things field. Its main products include industrial wireless routers, wireless data terminals, edge computing gateways, industrial Ethernet switches and other industrial Internet of things communication products, as well as smart distribution innovative solutions for the Internet of Things such as power grid status monitoring systems and smart vending control systems.

[5] The 1,446 companies here refer to the number of Zhongguancun NEEQ companies that disclosed their annual reports before April 30, 2017.

Table 1.3 Overview of the backdoor listing of Zhongguancun NEEQ companies

Rank	Before backdoor listing					After backdoor listing			
	Stock code	Name	Launch date	Delisting date	Listing place	Stock code	Name	Listing place	Launch date
1	834613.NQ	SINOHYTEC	2016-1-13	2020-6-18	Three boards	688339.SH	SINOHYTEC	Shanghai	2020-8-10
2	871196.NQ	BEIJING JIAODA SIGNAL TECHNOLOGY	2017-3-23	2020-4-21	Three boards	300851.SZ	BEIJING JIAODA SIGNAL TECHNOLOGY	Shenzhen	2020-7-17
3	430071.NQ	CDS	2010-8-2	2020-2-27	Three boards	300846.SZ	CDS	Shenzhen	2020-7-1
4	836019.NQ	IAT	2016-3-23	2020-1-16	Three boards	300825.SZ	IAT	Shenzhen	2020-3-27
5	430642.NQ	INHAND	2014-2-18	2020-1-15	Three boards	688080.SH	INHAND	Shanghai	2020-2-12
6	430581.NQ	BAYI SPACE	2014-1-24	2019-11-29	Three boards	688181.SH	BAYI SPACE	Shanghai	2020-1-6
7	430011.NQ	COMPASS	2007-1-23	2019-9-30	Three boards	300803.SZ	COMPASS	Shenzhen	2019-11-18
8	430002.NQ	SINOSOFT	2006-1-23	2019-8-1	Three boards	603927.SH	SINOSOFT	Shanghai	2019-9-9
9	832340.NQ	IBI	2015-4-23	2019-7-8	Three boards	603613.SH	IBI	Shanghai	2019-7-30
10	834291.NQ	CHINA CITIC PRESS	2015-11-26	2019-6-19	Three boards	300788.SZ	CHINA CITIC PRESS	Shenzhen	2019-7-5
11	835099.NQ	HAPPY TWIST	2015-12-29	2019-5-22	Three boards	A17178.SZ	HAPPY TWIST(IPO TERMINATED)	Shenzhen	–

(continued)

Table 1.3 (continued)

Rank	Before backdoor listing					After backdoor listing			
	Stock code	Name	Launch date	Delisting date	Listing place	Stock code	Name	Listing place	Launch date
12	836201.NQ	HE LI CHEN GUANG GROUP	2016-4-8	2019-4-23	Three boards	A16236.SZ	HE LI CHEN GUANG GROUP(IPO TERMINATED)	Shenzhen	–
13	834360.NQ	TINAVI	2015-11-19	2019-4-1	Three boards	688277.SH	TINAVI	Shanghai	2020-7-7
14	839570.NQ	ABT	2016-11-8	2019-3-5	Three boards	688168.SH	ABT	Shanghai	2019-9-6
15	835951.NQ	KE JING YUAN	2016-2-29	2018-12-19	Three boards	A09141.SZ	KE JING YUAN	Shenzhen	–
16	870077.NQ	PUPPY YOO	2016-12-6	2018-10-12	Three boards	A17383.SZ	PUPPY YOO(IPO TERMINATED)	Shenzhen	–
17	834391.NQ	LONGRUAN TECHNOLOGIES	2015-12-2	2018-10-10	Three boards	688078.SH	LONGRUAN TECHNOLOGIES	Shanghai	2019-12-30
18	832706.NQ	TIMELOIT	2015-7-6	2018-7-30	Three boards	A20440.SZ	TIMELOIT	Shenzhen	–
19	430243.NQ	TOPNEW INFO	2013-7-5	2018-6-6	Three boards	300895.SZ	TOPNEW INFO	Shenzhen	2020-9-24
20	836119.NQ	SUNNIWELL	2016-3-23	2018-5-21	Three boards	A11162.SZ	SUNNIWELL(IPOTERMINATED)	Shenzhen	–
21	871038.NQ	BROADV	2017-3-17	2018-1-25	Three boards	688004.SH	BROADV	Shanghai	2020-6-12

(continued)

Table 1.3 (continued)

Rank	Before backdoor listing					After backdoor listing			
	Stock code	Name	Launch date	Delisting date	Listing place	Stock code	Name	Listing place	Launch date
22	834801.NQ	TRICOLOR	2016-1-5	2018-1-19	Three boards	603516.SH	TRICOLOR	Shanghai	2018-2-2
23	833309.NQ	HCR	2015-8-12	2017-12-29	Three boards	688500.SH	HCR	Shanghai	2020-7-16
24	831008.NQ	BYBON	2014-8-29	2017-12-25	Three boards	300736.SZ	BYBON	Shenzhen	2018-1-9
25	832639.NQ	ZEHO	2015-6-16	2017-12-11	Three boards	A19351.SH	ZEHO	Shanghai	–
26	835686.NQ	BGT GROUP	2016-3-8	2017-11-17	Three boards	A19394.SZ	BGT GROUP	Shenzhen	–
27	831560.NQ	YJK BUILDING SOFTWARE	2014-12-25	2017-11-8	Three boards	300935.SZ	YJK BUILDING SOFTWARE	Shenzhen	2021-1-20
28	835079.NQ	ATA	2015-12-21	2017-10-11	Three boards	A18122.SH	ATA	Shanghai	–
29	835524.NQ	ZHONGYAN TECHNOLOGY	2016-1-18	2017-10-10	Three boards	003001.SZ	ZHONGYAN TECHNOLOGY	Shenzhen	2020-10-13
30	430162.NQ	JULI TECH	2012-11-2	2017-8-24	Three boards	A16121.SZ	JULI TECH(IPO TERMINATED)	Shenzhen	–
31	836285.NQ	DIANZHONG TECH	2016-3-14	2017-4-11	Three boards	A19224.SZ	DIANZHONG TECH	Shenzhen	–

(continued)

Table 1.3 (continued)

Rank	Before backdoor listing					After backdoor listing			
	Stock code	Name	Launch date	Delisting date	Listing place	Stock code	Name	Listing place	Launch date
32	835420.NQ	FENG SHANG SHI JI	2016-1-21	2017-3-21	Three boards	300860.SZ	FENG SHANG SHI JI	Shenzhen	2020-8-24
33	837493.NQ	PAPAYA	2016-5-16	2016-12-22	Three boards	A19041.SZ	PAPAYA	Shenzhen	–
34	835225.NQ	AT	2016-1-6	2016-12-5	Three boards	A19019.SH	AT (IPO TERMINATED)	Shanghai	–
35	430018.NQ	HEZONG	2007-9-19	2015-6-1	Three boards	300477.SZ	HEZONG	Shenzhen	2015-6-10
36	430040.NQ	CONST	2008-12-26	2015-4-22	Three boards	300445.SZ	CONST	Shenzhen	2015-4-24
37	430049.NQ	SOJO	2009-2-18	2015-4-20	Three boards	300444.SZ	SOJO	Shenzhen	2015-4-23
38	430,045.NQ	KYLAND	2009-2-18	2012-8-29	Three boards	300353.SZ	KYLAND	Shenzhen	2012-9-27
39	430012.NQ	BOHUI INNOVATION	2007-2-16	2012-5-10	Three boards	300318.SZ	BOHUI INNOVATION	Shenzhen	2012-5-23
40	430008.NQ	THUNISOFT	2006-8-30	2011-9-28	Three boards	300271.SZ	THUNISOFT	Shenzhen	2011-10-26
41	430023.NQ	JXFH	2007-10-26	2011-4-20	Three boards	300213.SZ	JXFH	Shenzhen	2011-5-5

(continued)

Table 1.3 (continued)

Rank	Before backdoor listing					After backdoor listing			
	Stock code	Name	Launch date	Delisting date	Listing place	Stock code	Name	Listing place	Launch date
42	430001.NQ	IREAL	2006-1-23	2010-12-6	Three boards	300150.SZ	IREAL	Shenzhen	2010-12-22
43	430006.NQ	BEILU PHARMA	2006-8-28	2009-9-30	Three boards	300016.SZ	BEILU PHARMA	Shenzhen	2009-10-30
44	430007.NQ	JOIN-CHEER	2006-9-7	2009-7-29	Three boards	002279.SZ	JOIN-CHEER	Shenzhen	2009-8-11

Note "—" means Wind has not made clear statistics yet
Source Wind, compiled by ZLCA.

in clearing out inferior enterprises and improving the quality of Zhongguancun NEEQ Companies.

Second, the NEEQ reform made that the threshold for investors has been lowered and corporate liquidity has been eased to a certain extent. In October 2019, the China Securities Regulatory Commission announced the comprehensive deepening reform of the NEEQ. Subsequently, the threshold for qualified investors in the NEEQ has also dropped significantly. The investment thresholds for the basic layer, innovation layer, and selection layer were lowered to 2 million yuan, 1.5 million yuan, and 1 million yuan respectively. According to data released by the National Equity Exchange Corporation, as of the end of 2020, the number of qualified investor accounts in the New Third Board market reached 1,658,200,[6] which is 7.2 times that of the end of 2019. The increase in the number of qualified investors has greatly improved the liquidity of the new third board market, and to a certain extent alleviated the difficulties of corporate financing and the small volume of stock transactions, and the willingness of companies to delist is relatively weakened.

1.1.2 The Industry[7] Is Widely Distributed, Focusing on Information Technology, Industry and Service Industries

Over 60% of enterprises are distributed in Information transmission, Software and IT services and manufacturing. Among them, the number of Information transmission, Software and IT services is 363, accounting for 39.80%; the number of Manufacturing is 201, accounting for 22.04%. In addition, Leasing and Business services, Scientific research and technology service, Wholesale and Retail businesses, Culture, Sports and Entertainment are also involved (Table 1.4).

1.1.3 NEEQ Liquidity Bottomed Out and the Number of Shareholders Skyrocketed

1.1.3.1 Changes in the Number of Shareholders

Since the reform of the NEEQ, the liquidity of the NEEQ companies' stocks has been improved to a certain extent. After excluding new companies in 2019 and 2020, the number of shareholders of 372 Zhongguancun NEEQ companies has increased to varying degrees in 2020. Among them, the number of shareholders of 155 companies

[6] There were 57,400 institutional investors and 1,600,800 individual investors.

[7] The industry classification in this article is based on the "Results of Management Classification of Listed Companies" published by the NEEQ.

Table 1.4 Industry distribution of Zhongguancun NEEQ companies (Unit: Number, %)

Industry	Amount	Ratio
Information transmission, Software and IT services	363	39.80
Manufacturing	201	22.04
Leasing and Business services	83	9.10
Scientific research and technology service	58	6.36
Wholesale and Retail businesses	52	5.70
Culture, Sports and Entertainment	52	5.70
Education	23	2.52
Management of Water Conservancy, Environment and Public Facilities	22	2.41
Construction	17	1.86
Financials	9	0.99
Transportation, Warehousing and Postal services	7	0.77
Mining	5	0.55
Electricity, Heat, Gas and Water production and supply industry	5	0.55
Residential services, Repairs and other services	5	0.55
Health and Social work	5	0.55
Real Estate	3	0.33
Agriculture, Forestry, Animal husbandry and Fishery	1	0.11
Accommodation and Catering industry	1	0.11
Total	912	100.00

Source Wind, compiled by ZLCA

has increased for two consecutive years. A detailed analysis of these companies shows that in 2020, the number of new shareholders of 155 companies was 173 thousand, which was 54.47 times of that in 2019. After excluding Select Companies, the remaining companies still added 12,200 shareholders (Table 1.5). Judging from the median and maximum number of new shareholders, companies will have obvious advantages in terms of the number of new shareholders in 2020 (Table 1.5). From

Table 1.5 The situation of 155 Zhongguancun NEEQ companies that have increased the number of shareholders for two consecutive years from 2019 to 2020

	Number of new shareholders in 2019	Number of new shareholders in 2020
Total number	3175	172,955
Total number of excluding Select Companies	3175	12,244
Median number	5	21
Maximum number	424	57,195

Source Wind, compiled by ZLCA

the change of the number of shareholders of a single enterprise, 36 enterprises have increased the number of shareholders by no less than 100 for two consecutive years (Table 1.6).

1.1.3.2 Stock Issuance and Trading

Stock Issuance

In 2020, Zhongguancun's NEEQ Companies stock issuance bottomed out and rebounded. There were 82 stock issuances throughout the year, an increase of 3.80% year-on-year; the total financing scale was 5.979 billion yuan, an increase of 45.86% year-on-year; the average single financing amount was 73 million yuan, an increase of 40.38% year-on-year (Table 1.7).

Stock Trading

The stock liquidity of Zhongguancun NEEQ Listed Companies has increased for three consecutive years. In 2020, a total of 568 Zhongguancun NEEQ companies participated in stock transactions, an increase of 6.17% compared with 535 in 2019. The annual stock trading volume was 3.814 billion shares, and the turnover was 19.166 billion yuan. Both increased significantly compared with 2019 (Fig. 1.4). Among them, the stock trading volume was 2.20 times that of 2019; the turnover was 4.52 times that of 2019; the average stock trading price was twice that of 2019. The stock liquidity of Zhongguancun's NEEQ Companies has increased significantly.

Stock trading volume presents an obvious head effect. From the perspective of trading scale, among Zhongguancun NEEQ Listed Companies in 2020, there are 29 companies with an annual trading volume of not less than 100 million yuan, and their total trading size is 17,071 billion yuan, accounting for 89.06% of the transaction volume; There are 361 companies with an annual turnover of 78 million yuan, accounting for only 0.41%. In addition, the number of enterprises with no trading volume within a year is 505, accounting for 47.06% of the total number of Zhongguancun NEEQ Listed Companies, which is nearly half (Table 1.8).

From the perspective of trading methods, companies that adopt Continuous Call Auction trading have great advantages in terms of trading activity, average trading volume, and average trading price. Specifically, the stock trading volume of the 7 companies with Continuous Call Auction trading is not 0; out of 78 companies that use Market Making trading, only 2 companies have 0 stock trading volumes; there are 988 companies that use Call Auction trading, but only 485 companies have stock trading volume, accounting for less than half. In terms of average turnover, the average turnover of companies that adopt Continuous Call Auction trading is 803 million yuan, far exceeding the 118-million-yuan average turnover of Market Making trading enterprises and that of 9-million-yuan average turnover of Collective Call Auction trading enterprises. In terms of average trading price, Continuous Call

Table 1.6 Zhongguancun NEEQ companies with an increase in the number of shareholders for two consecutive years and no less than 100 shareholders in 2020

Rank	Stock code	Name	Classification	Number of shareholders (2018)	Number of shareholders (2019)	Number of shareholders (2020)	Number of increase of shareholders in 2020 compared to 2019
1	833819.NQ	NUTRICHEM	Select	104	166	57,361	57,195
2	835184.NQ	GRAND TECH	Select	119	136	41,276	41,140
3	836263.NQ	ZHTD	Select	31	52	27,630	27,578
4	832317.NQ	SKYCAM	Select	226	252	24,692	24,440
5	430047.NQ	NORTHLAND	Select	152	202	10,560	10,358
6	430193.NQ	WIN MEDIA	Select	56	93	1,124	1,031
7	830815.NQ	BLUE MOUNTAINS TECHNOLOGY	Innovation	799	842	1,718	876
8	430046.NQ	SBR INFORMATION	Innovation	137	227	958	731
9	834082.NQ	CNBM TECHNOLOGY CO.,LTD	Innovation	114	538	1,231	693
10	430005.NQ	HTA	Innovation	640	746	1,370	624
11	833575.NQ	HEALTH GUARD	Base	23	97	710	613
12	836346.NQ	EMAR	Innovation	71	253	841	588
13	430075.NQ	ZXSF	Innovation	584	656	1,089	433
14	832646.NQ	COMMCHINA	Innovation	108	149	505	356
15	430208.NQ	UXSINO	Innovation	561	761	1,090	329

(continued)

Table 1.6 (continued)

Rank	Stock code	Name	Classification	Number of shareholders (2018)	Number of shareholders (2019)	Number of shareholders (2020)	Number of increase of shareholders in 2020 compared to 2019
16	837592.NQ	YONDERVISION	Innovation	28	39	328	289
17	836964.NQ	HTHS	Innovation	56	63	331	268
18	832924.NQ	BRIGHTSTONE	Innovation	73	169	421	252
19	430267.NQ	SHENGSHI QUANTUM	Innovation	93	156	371	215
20	430375.NQ	STAR CUBE	Innovation	137	181	381	200
21	831142.NQ	EASTED	Innovation	237	247	434	187
22	430017.NQ	SUNHO	Innovation	115	170	344	174
23	430021.NQ	HISIGN TECHNOLOGY	Innovation	308	349	522	173
24	430074.NQ	GSIT	Innovation	443	527	679	152
25	835179.NQ	KAIDE QUARTZ	Innovation	14	16	156	140
26	430182.NQ	AEBIZ	Innovation	96	97	236	139
27	833044.NQ	HEAVEN-SENT CAPITAL MANAGEMENT	Base	914	993	1,129	136
28	839483.NQ	YONYOU FINANCIAL INFORMATION TECHNOLOGY	Innovation	21	48	183	135
29	872808.NQ	SUGON	Innovation	16	22	155	133

(continued)

Table 1.6 (continued)

Rank	Stock code	Name	Classification	Number of shareholders (2018)	Number of shareholders (2019)	Number of shareholders (2020)	Number of increase of shareholders in 2020 compared to 2019
30	430094.NQ	CHIPADVANCED	Base	48	49	182	133
31	833175.NQ	HAOHAN DATA	Base	26	29	158	129
32	833966.NQ	TECHNOLOGY & INVESTMENT	Innovation	15	17	141	124
33	870381.NQ	BEIJING 797 AUDIO	Innovation	33	38	160	122
34	832028.NQ	HUIYUAN NETWORK	Innovation	285	391	504	113
35	834777.NQ	I&G	Base	254	330	432	102
36	836885.NQ	HEADSPRING	Innovation	35	69	170	101

Source Wind, compiled by ZLCA

Table 1.7 2016–2020 Zhongguancun NEEQ stock issuance status

Year	Stock issuance		Financing		Average financing	
	Amount (time)	Growth rate (%)	Amount (hundred million)	Growth rate (%)	Amount (hundred million)	Growth rate (%)
2016	511	17.20	343.06	3.57	0.67	−11.63
2017	419	−18.00	276.1	−19.52	0.66	−1.85
2018	186	− 55.61	83.01	−69.93	0.45	−32.27
2019	79	−57.53	40.99	−50.62	0.52	15.30
2020	82	3.80%	59.79	45.86	0.73	40.38

Source 2020 NEEQ Market Statistics Express, compiled by ZLCA

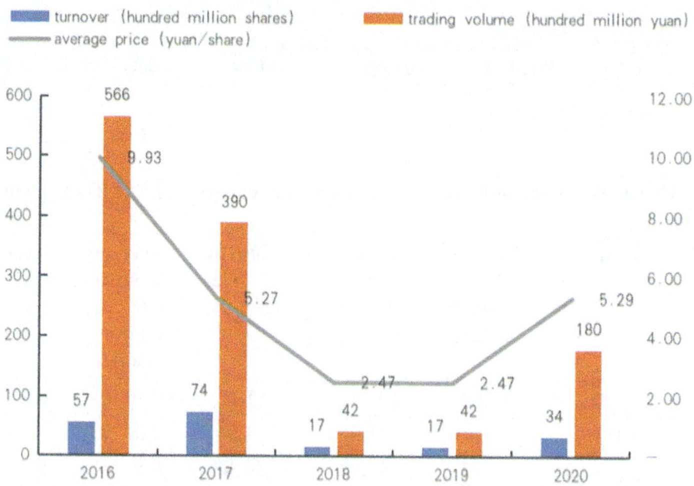

Fig. 1.4 The changes in annual sttock trading volume and turnover of Zhongguancun NEEQ companies in 2016–2020 (*Source* Wind, compiled by ZLCA)

Table 1.8 Distribution of trading volumen of Zhongguancun NEEQ companies in 2020

	Enterprises (Amount)	Total turnover (100 million yuan)	Ratio of total turnover (%)
≥100 million	29	170.71	89.06
50 million–100 million	11	7.29	3.80
10 million–50 million	38	8.65	4.51
5 million–10 million	27	1.92	1.00
1 million–5 million	102	2.32	1.21
<1 million	361	0.78	0.41

Source Wind, compiled by ZLCA

Table 1.9 The stock trading volume of Zhongguancun NEEQ companies in different trading methods in 2020

Trading methods	Amount	Volume (100 million shares)	Turnover (100 million yuan)	Ratio of turnover (%)	Average turnover (100 million yuan)	Average trading price (yuan/share)
Collective Call Auction trading	485	13.84	45.57	23.78	0.09	3.29
Continuous Call Auction trading	7	6.42	56.23	29.34	8.03	8.76
Market Making trading	76	17.88	89.85	46.88	1.18	5.03
In total	568	38.14	191.65	100.00	0.34	5.02

Source Wind, compiled by ZLCA

Table 1.10 The stock trading volume of different market classification of Zhongguancun NEEQ companies in 2020

Market classification	Amount	Volume (100 million shares)	Turnover (100 million yuan)	Ratio of turnover (%)	Average turnover (100 million yuan)	Average trading price (yuan/share)
Innovation	150	17.62	109.47	57.12	0.73	6.21
Base	411	14.1	25.96	13.54	0.06	1.84
Select	7	6.42	56.23	29.34	8.03	8.76
In total	568	38.14	191.66	100.00	0.34	5.03

Source Wind, compiled by ZLCA

Auction trading also has a huge advantage. Its average trading price is 1.74 times that of Market Making trading and 2.66 times that of Collective Call Auction trading (Table 1.9).

From the angle of market classification, Select companies have obvious advantages in trading activity and average trading prices. In terms of trading activity, the stock trading volume of the 7 Select companies is not 0; of the 151 Innovation companies, only 1 company has a stock trading volume of 0; and the number of Base companies has stock trading is 411, accounting for 53.52% of the total Base companies. In terms of average trading volume and average trading price, Select companies' advantages are also very obvious (Table 1.10).

From the angle of industry distribution, the average trading volume of Financials, Scientific Research and Technology Service, Manufacturing, Transportation, Warehousing and Postal services, Information Transmission, Software and IT services,

Management of Water Conservancy, Environment and Public Facilities are all over 10 million. The average turnover of Financials is close to 100 million. From the perspective of average trading price, that of the six industries is higher than the average, of which that of Scientific Research and Technology Service and Health and Social work all exceed 10 yuan per share (Table 1.11).

Thanks to the comprehensive and deepening reform of the NEEQ, the liquidity of Zhongguancun NEEQ enterprises has increased significantly. The main reasons are as follows:

First, the threshold for investors has been lowered. The NEEQ investor threshold has been lowered from 5 million before the comprehensive deepening reform to 1 million of Select, 1.5 million of Innovation and 2 million of Base as the individual investor access standards, which meets the investment preferences of different investors; the second is introducing public funds to clarify the specific transaction types and methods of QFII and RQFII in the NEEQ investment. A series of reform measures have brought resources to the NEEQ companies and effectively promoted the liquidity of NEEQ companies. Data shows that by the end of 2020, the number of qualified investor accounts in NEEQ reached 1,658,200, including 57,400 institutional investors and 1,600,800 individual investors. The number of qualified investors is 7.2 times that of the end of 2019.

The second is to set up Select and implement a public offering system. For companies that have been listed on the NEEQ for twelve consecutive months, if they meet the public offering conditions and enter the Select conditions, they can apply for the public offering and enter the Select. The number of shareholders of the Select company in the public offering shall be no less than 200. In 2020, there are 7 Zhongguancun NEEQ companies that will enter the Select public offering, the number of shareholders of which totaled 209,400 and this number was only 1,062 at the end of 2019.

The third is the change of trading rules. (1) The number of stock declaration declined. From March 30st, 2020, the NEEQ will fully implement the "National Equities Exchange And Quotations Stock Trading Rules", the minimum number of single declarations will be lowered from 1,000 shares to 100 shares, the minimum trading unit requirement will be cancelled. It will be released that the number of single declarations must be an integer multiple of 100 shares to reduce the cost of a single trading for investors; (2) The frequency of matching is increased. Combining the equity dispersion and liquidity needs of listed companies in different market levels, the Continuous Call Auction trading method was launched in Select. The frequency of Collective Call Auction matching in Base was increased to 5 times per day, and that of Innovation was increased to 25 times per day.

Table 1.11 The stock trading volume of Zhongguancun NEEQ companies in various industries in 2020

Industries	Amount	Volume (ten thousand shares)	Turnover (ten thousand yuan)	Average of turnover (ten thousand yuan)	Average trading price (yuan/share)
Financials	5	65,740.04	49,927.19	9,985.44	0.76
Scientific research and technology service	33	19,987.25	213,356.94	6,465.36	10.67
Manufacturing	127	140,106.05	766,711.12	6,037.10	5472.36
Transportation, Warehousing and Postal services	3	23,008.64	11,503.67	3,834.56	0.50
Information transmission, Software and IT services	235	110,726.77	822,493.10	3,499.97	7.43
Management of Water Conservancy, Environment and Public Facilities	17	4,655.28	27,360.40	1,609.44	5.88
Construction	13	1,635.76	4,424.72	340.36	2.70
Education	17	2,150.66	4,035.28	237.37	1.88
Leasing and Business services	48	6,363.60	11,082.07	230.88	1.74
Electricity, Heat, Gas and Water production and supply industry	2	2,494.98	397.32	198.66	0.16
Health and Social work	2	16.55	247.57	123.79	14.96
Culture, Sports and Entertainment	33	3,132.90	3,439.35	104.22	1.10
Wholesale and Retail businesses	28	1,317.06	2,721.62	97.20	2.07
Real Estate	2	169.97	156.60	78.30	0.92

(continued)

Table 1.11 (continued)

Industries	Amount	Volume (ten thousand shares)	Turnover (ten thousand yuan)	Average of turnover (ten thousand yuan)	Average trading price (yuan/share)
Residential services, Repairs and other services	1	27.99	40.99	40.99	1.46
Mining	3	9.41	11.88	3.96	1.26
In total	568	381,345.54	1,916,605.60	3,374.31	5.03

Source Wind, compiled by ZLCA

1.1.4 Select Raised Funds Over 2.2 Billion Yuan and Private Enterprises Still Have Difficulties in Issuing Bonds

Compared with listed companies, NEEQ Listed Companies have relatively narrow financing channels due to their smaller asset scale and unstable growth. Currently, NEEQ Listed Companies can raise financing through bank credit, Select Public Issuance of Stocks, Equity Private Placement, Corporate Bond, Market Making System, Preferred Stocks, and Equity Pledges. Since data related to some financing methods cannot be obtained through public channels, this report only analyzes the financing status of Zhongguancun NEEQ companies in 2020 through Equity Private Placement, Corporate Bond.

1.1.4.1 Public Offering

In 2020, the first batch of 7 Zhongguancun NEEQ companies successfully listed on Select, raising funds to reach 2.288 billion yuan. Among them, NUTRICHEM (545 million yuan) raised the most funds (Tables 1.12 and 1.13).

1.1.4.2 Equity Private Placement

Generally speaking, companies can use Equity Private Placement to raise funds while applying for listing or after listing. The company's Equity Private Placement of stocks uses a one-time application and issuance in installments, which simplifies the review procedures for stock issuance. The funds raised by this way need to be used for special purposes, and the supervision method is relatively strict. It can usually be used to supplement working capital, repay bank loans and other debts, project financing, equity incentives, asset acquisitions and other matters.

In the past five years, the number and frequency of Equity Private Placement and the actual scale of funds raised have continued to decline, but the decline has

Table 1.12 Zhongguancun NEEQ companies with a stock turnover of Over 100 million yuan in 2020

Rank	Stock Code	Name	Company Property	Classification	Industry	Trading Method	Annual average turnover rate (%)	Volumen (100 million shares)	Turnover (100 million yuan)
1	834082.NQ	CNBM TECHNOLOGY CO.,LTD	State-owned enterprises	Innovation	Information transmission, Software and IT services	Market Making trading	56.24	0.84	25.81
2	832317.NQ	SKYCAM	Private enterprises	Select	Scientific research and technology service	Continuous Call Auction trading	213.22	1.39	20.07
3	833819.NQ	NUTRICHEM	Private enterprises	Select	Manufacturing	Continuous Call Auction trading	73.77	2.10	12.39
4	833575.NQ	HEALTH GUARD	Private enterprises	Base	Manufacturing	Market Making trading	53.11	0.38	11.91
5	430005.NQ	HTA	State-owned enterprises	Innovation	Manufacturing	Collective Call Auction trading	15.65	0.23	10.35
6	430047.NQ	NORTHLAND	Private enterprises	Select	Manufacturing	Continuous Call Auction trading	84.33	1.04	8.02
7	430075.NQ	ZXSF	Private enterprises	Innovation	Manufacturing	Market Making trading	166.10	2.22	7.32

(continued)

Table 1.12 (continued)

Rank	Stock Code	Name	Company Property	Classification	Industry	Trading Method	Annual average turnover rate (%)	Volumen (100 million shares)	Turnover (100 million yuan)
8	430193.NQ	WIN MEDIA	Public enterprises	Innovation	Information transmission, Software and IT services	Collective Call Auction trading	126.18	0.66	7.09
9	836346.NQ	EMAR	Private enterprises	Innovation	Information transmission, Software and IT services	Market Making trading	159.09	0.90	5.97
10	830815.NQ	BLUE MOUNTAINS TECHNOLOGY	Private enterprises	Innovation	Manufacturing	Market Making trading	251.30	2.93	5.69
11	430046.NQ	SBR INFORMATION	Private enterprises	Innovation	Information transmission, Software and IT services	Market Making trading	76.65	0.66	5.46
12	430208.NQ	UXSINO	Private enterprises	Innovation	Information transmission, Software and IT services	Market Making trading	21.56	0.38	5.29
13	835184.NQ	GRAND TECH	Private enterprises	Select	Information transmission, Software and IT services	Continuous Call Auction trading	80.50	0.46	4.72
14	836964.NQ	HTHS	Private enterprises	Innovation	Manufacturing	Market Making trading	261.07	1.55	4.57

(continued)

Table 1.12 (continued)

Rank	Stock Code	Name	Company Property	Classification	Industry	Trading Method	Annual average turnover rate (%)	Volumen (100 million shares)	Turnover (100 million yuan)
15	835508.NQ	IN-TO	Private enterprises	Select	Information transmission, Software and IT services	Continuous Call Auction trading	196.70	0.34	4.54
16	834021.NQ	GOLDEN TIMES	Private enterprises	Select	Information transmission, Software and IT services	Continuous Call Auction trading	56.04	0.69	4.05
17	430719.NQ	TCJDCAPITAL	Private enterprises	Base	Financials	Collective Call Auction trading	3.84	5.59	4.00
18	430074.NQ	GSIT	Private enterprises	Innovation	Manufacturing	Market Making trading	33.10	0.36	3.75
19	837344.NQ	TRI-PRIME GENE	Private enterprises	Innovation	Manufacturing	Collective Call Auction trading	20.40	0.10	2.81
20	839483.NQ	YONYOU FINANCIAL INFORMATION TECHNOLOGY	Private enterprises	Innovation	Information transmission, Software and IT services	Market Making trading	14.67	0.15	2.74
21	832924.NQ	BRIGHTSTONE	Private enterprises	Innovation	Manufacturing	Collective Call Auction trading	7.11	1.24	2.53

(continued)

Table 1.12 (continued)

Rank	Stock Code	Name	Company Property	Classification	Industry	Trading Method	Annual average turnover rate (%)	Volumen (100 million shares)	Turnover (100 million yuan)
22	836263.NQ	ZHTD	Private enterprises	Select	Management of Water Conservancy, Environment and Public Facilities	Continuous Call Auction trading	66.39	0.40	2.45
23	430021.NQ	HISIGN TECHNOLOGY	Private enterprises	Innovation	Information transmission, Software and IT services	Market Making trading	35.14	0.53	1.89
24	430017.NQ	SUNHO	Private enterprises	Innovation	Manufacturing	Collective Call Auction trading	9.74	0.09	1.46
25	430090.NQ	BJB	Private enterprises	Innovation	Information transmission, Software and IT services	Collective Call Auction trading	45.32	0.33	1.31
26	836577.NQ	HUAHONG TECHNOLOGY	Private enterprises	Base	Information transmission, Software and IT services	Collective Call Auction trading	17.72	0.01	1.25
27	870381.NQ	BEIJING 797 AUDIO	State-owned enterprises	Innovation	Manufacturing	Market Making trading	37.18	0.05	1.18

(continued)

Table 1.12 (continued)

Rank	Stock Code	Name	Company Property	Classification	Industry	Trading Method	Annual average turnover rate (%)	Volumen (100 million shares)	Turnover (100 million yuan)
28	430330.NQ	ICPC	Private enterprises	Innovation	Information transmission, Software and IT services	Market Making trading	39.48	0.27	1.07
29	831900.NQ	HNA COLD CHAIN	other enterprises	Base	Transportation, Warehousing and Postal services	Market Making trading	19.60	2.27	1.05

Source Wind, compiled by ZLCA

Table 1.13 Public offerings of select companies on the Zhongguancun NEEQ in 2020 (Unit: 100 million yuan)

Rank	Wind Code	Name	Launch Date	Industry	Scale of raised funds
1	833819.NQ	NUTRICHEM	2020-07-27	Manufacturing	5.45
2	832317.NQ	SKYCAM	2020-07-27	Scientific research and technology service	5.42
3	835184.NQ	GRAND TECH	2020-07-27	Information transmission, Software and IT services	3.97
4	430047.NQ	NORTHLAND	2020-11-24	Manufacturing	2.48
5	836263.NQ	ZHTD	2020-07-27	Management of Water Conservancy, Environment and Public Facilities	2.41
6	834021.NQ	GOLDEN TIMES	2020-07-27	Information transmission, Software and IT services	2.15
7	835508.NQ	IN-TO	2020-07-27	Information transmission, Software and IT services	1.00

Source Wind, compiled by ZLCA

continued to slow down, and the average scale of single funds raised has also fallen slightly. In the whole year of 2020, a total of 552 NEEQ listed companies across the country have implemented 581 Equity Private Placement, and the actual fundraising scale is 19.773 billion yuan, with an average single fundraising scale of 34.03 million yuan. Among them, 64 Zhongguancun NEEQ Listed Companies have implemented 65 Equity Private Placement, and the actual scale of funds raised is 3.589 billion yuan, accounting for 18.15% of the national NEEQ Listed Companies' Equity Private Placement funds raised, and the average single-fund raising scale is 55.22 million yuan, which is 62.27% higher than that of national NEEQ listed company (Table 1.14).

In terms of the purpose of issuance, the purpose of 60 companies' Equity Private Placement is to supplement liquidity; financing of 2 companies is for the acquisition of other assets; each respectively is for inter-company asset replacement and reorganization, equity incentives, and actual controller asset injection (Table 1.15).

According to statistics on the scale of funds raised through Equity Private Placement, the median amount of funds raised through such method in 2020 is 13.746 million yuan. Among them, 8 times have actually raised funds of more than 100

Table 1.14 Funds raised by Equity Private Placement of Zhongguancun NEEQ listed companies 2015–2020

Year	The number of enterprise	Number of additional issuance (times)	The actual scale of funds raised	Number of additional shares	Average single fundraising scale
			(100 million yuan)	(100 million shares)	(ten thousand yuan)
2015	283	376	309.62	55.84	8235
2016	404	461	284.54	61.75	6172
2017	342	377	227.23	26.74	6027
2018	134	144	47.14	8.36	3274
2019	64	67	37.40	7.00	5582
2020	64	65	35.89	6.92	5522

Source Wind, compiled by ZLCA

Table 1.15 The purpose of Equity Private Placement of Zhongguancun NEEQ listed companies in 2020

The purpose of Equity Private Placement	Number of enterprise
supplement liquidity	60
inter-company asset replacement and reorganization	1
equity incentives	1
acquisition of other assets	2
actual controller asset injection	1
In total	65

Source Wind, compiled by ZLCA

million yuan through private placement, and the actual total funds raised was 2.610 billion yuan, accounting for 72.74%. The number of companies with actual fundraising scales of not less than 100 million yuan increased by 2 compared with last year. There are 5 times for companies with 50 million to 100 million yuan, and the actual total amount of funds raised is 289 million yuan; 40 times for companies with 10 million to 50 million yuan, and the actual total amount of funds raised is 641 million yuan; there are 12 companies with financing less than 10 million yuan and the actual total amount of funds raised was 48 million yuan (Table 1.16).

From the angle of market classification, Innovation companies implemented a total of 32 Equity Private Placement and issued 149 million additional shares. The total amount of funds raised was 1.376 billion yuan, and the average single fundraising scale was 43.0 million yuan; Base companies implemented 33 Equity Private Placement, a total of 543 million additional shares were issued, the total amount of funds raised was 2.212 billion yuan, and the average size of a single fundraising was 670.303 billion yuan. The reason why the Base company's financing scale is higher

Table 1.16 Statistics on the scale of funds raised by Equity Private Placement of Zhongguancun NEEQ listed companies in 2020

Equity Private Placement financing range	Equity Private Placement frequency		Total financing	
	frequency (times)	Ratio (%)	Total amount (100 million yuan)	Ratio (%)
≥100 million yuan	8	12.31	26.10	72.74
50 million yuan–100 million yuan	5	7.69	2.89	8.05
10 million yuan–50 million yuan	40	61.54	6.41	17.87
<10 million yuan	12	18.46	0.48	1.34

Source: Wind, compiled by ZLCA

Table 1.17 A hierarchical comparison of funds raised by Equity Private Placement of Zhongguancun NEEQ listed companies in 2020

Classification	Additional enterprise	Additional shares	Scale of raised funds	Scale of average single fundraising
	(times)	(100 million shares)	(100 million yuan)	(10 thousand yuan)
Innovation	32	1.49	13.76	4,300.00
Base	33	5.43	22.12	6,703.03

Source Wind, compiled by ZLCA

than that of Innovation is that 5 companies with a financing scale of no less than 100 million yuan have a total financing scale of 1.756 billion yuan,[8] to a certain extent, the total financing scale and average financing scale of Base have been improved (Table 1.17). Among the Innovation companies, only three have a financing scale of no less than 100 million yuan, and these three companies have raised a total of 854 million yuan (Table 1.18).

1.1.4.3 Corporate Bond Issuance Status

In 2020, the total issuance of corporate bond by national NEEQ listed companies was 9.120 billion yuan. Among them, three Zhongguancun NEEQ Listed Companies issued three corporate bonds, with a scale of 3.65 billion yuan, accounting for 40.02% of that in the national total NEEQ listed companies. Specifically, in 2020, the scale of corporate bonds issued by Zhongguancun NEEQ Listed Companies was 3.65 billion

[8] The scale of fundraising of HEALTH GUARD, Zhongguancun NEEQ enterprise in Base, is 650 million yuan; that of BCEG ADVABCED CONSTRUCTION MATERIALS is 400 million yuan; that of Huaru is 298 million yuan; the scale of CIVIGAS is 207 million yuan; XINGZHI' fund-raising scale is 200 million yuan.

Table 1.18 Statistics of Zhongguancun NEEQ listed companies with a scale of 100 million yuan or more in Equity Private Placement in 2020

rank	stock code	name	classification	Industry	issuance price	Number of additional issuance (ten thousand shares)	Total actual fundraising (ten thousand yuan)	Purpose of additional issuance
1	833575.NQ	HEALTH GUARD	Base	Manufacturing	19.70	3,300.00	65,010.00	supplement liquidity
2	430005.NQ	HTA	Innovation	Manufacturing	21.00	2,922.41	61,370.69	supplement liquidity
3	872287.NQ	BCEG ADVABCED CONSTRUCTION MATERIALS	Base	Manufacturing	5.03	7,952.29	40,000.00	supplement liquidity
4	837069.NQ	HUARU	Base	Information transmission, Software and IT services	26.53	1,124.00	29,819.72	supplement liquidity
5	871892.NQ	CIVIGAS	Base	Electricity, Heat, Gas and Water production and supply industry	1.00	20,742.00	20,742.00	inter-company asset replacement and reorganization
6	831027.NQ	XINGZHI	Base	Education	2.00	10,000.00	20,000.00	supplement liquidity
7	833024.NQ	XINZHIHENG	Innovation	Information transmission, Software and IT services	7.97	1,617.00	12,887.49	supplement liquidity
8	835179.NQ	KAIDE QUARTZ	Innovation	Manufacturing	13.00	860.00	11,180.00	supplement liquidity

Source Wind, compiled by ZLCA

Table 1.19 Corporate bond issuance of Zhongguancun NEEQ companies in 2020

Bond code	Name	Industry attributes	Issuance scale (100 million)	Issuance period (year)	Coupon rate (%)	Use of raised funds
175051.SH	I&G	State-owned enterprises	30.00	3.00	4.47	It is intended to be used to repay interest-bearing debts, optimize debt structure, supplement working capital, etc
166668.SH	CAPITAL AIR	State-owned enterprises	1.50	3.00	4.00	It is intended to be used to repay the company's interest-bearing debts and supplement the company's working capital
166190.SH	CKFIL	Public enterprises	5.00	3.00	6.50	It is planned to use 120 million yuan to provide support to relevant enterprises for epidemic prevention work to invest in direct lease projects; 880 million yuan will be used to repay debts

Source: Wind, compiled by ZLCA

yuan, and the bond issuance period will be 3 years; the interest rate of most corporate bonds will be between 4.00% and 6.50%. From the perspective of company attributes, the three companies issuing corporate bonds are all state-owned enterprises (Table 1.19).

1.1.5 The COVID-19 Affects Corporate Profits, But More Than 30% of Companies Keep Growth

In early 2020, the unexpected outbreak and spread of the COVID-19 delayed the company's resumption of work and production and disrupted the company's original

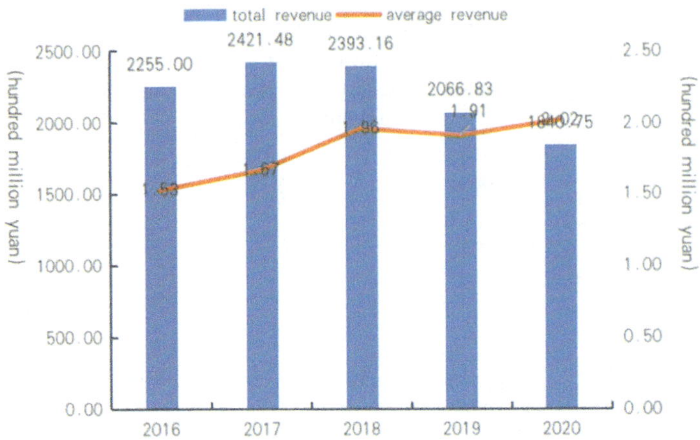

Fig. 1.5 Changes in total revenue and average revenue of Zhongguancun NEEQ companies From 2016 to 2020 (*Source* Wind, compiled by ZLCA

production and operation arrangements. In this context, the government has introduced a series of tax and fee reduction measures to "reduce the burden" on enterprises and ensure the orderly resumption of work and production. The promulgation of a series of policies has effectively stimulated the vitality of enterprises, but the operating performance of the gathering consumer service industries such as Wholesale and Retail businesses, Education, Transportation, Catering industry, Culture, Sports and Entertainment, and the employee-intensive Manufacturing industries are still affected.

Affected by the pandemia and the decrease in the number of NEEQ companies, the total operating income and net profit of Zhongguancun NEEQ companies in 2020 shows a downward trend, but the overall quality has steadily improved. In this year, the total operating income of Zhongguancun NEEQ companies was 18.475 billion yuan, a year-on-year decrease of 10.94% (Fig. 1.5), and the average operating income was 202 million yuan, a year-on-year increase of 5.76%. In addition, from 2019 to 2020, the total operating income of companies with continuing operations in 2020 will be 182.615 billion yuan, a year-on-year decrease of 2.99%.

In 2020, the total net profit of Zhongguancun NEEQ Companies was 1.541 billion yuan, a year-on-year decrease of 81.06%; the average net profit was 1,689,700 yuan, a year-on-year decrease of 77.55%. The reason is that the three companies with serious losses have lowered the overall net profit of Zhongguancun NEEQ Companies. Among them, CAPITAL HELICOPTER (832494.NQ) which provide diversified general aviation services and airport services, had the highest loss in 2020 under the influence of the epidemic and the group's bankruptcy and reorganization process, reaching 2.610 billion yuan; CHINAEQUITY (833858.NQ), one of the first independent institutions of venture capital and private equity investment in China, due to the business transformation of its holding subsidiary Hifuture Technology in 2020, the launch time of game products has been delayed, and the company has

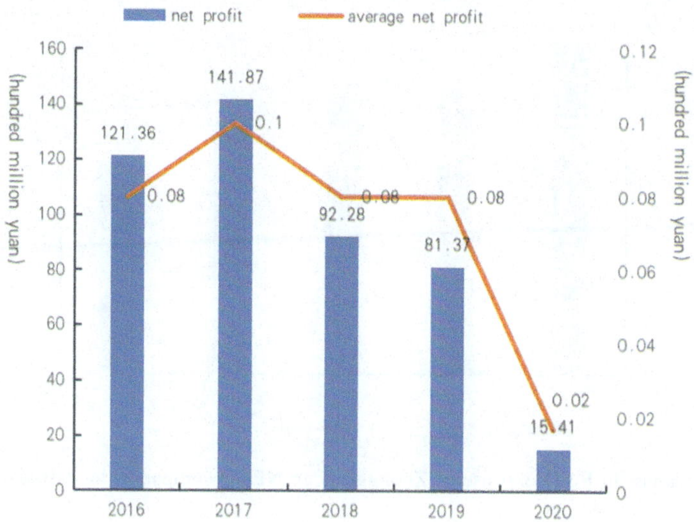

Fig. 1.6 Changes in total net profit and average net profit of Zhongguancun NEEQ companies from 2016 to 2020 (*Source* Wind, compiled by ZLCA)

not been able to contribute revenue to the company as scheduled. The company made goodwill impairment (a total of 1.658 billion yuan) provisions for its holding subsidiaries Hifuture Technology and DKMgame, resulting in a relatively high loss of 2.474 billion yuan; HNA Cold Chain (831900.NQ), which is committed to third-party cold chain logistics warehousing, transportation, and distribution services, has completely ceased its procurement and execution business mainly for cross-border fresh food due to the pandemia. In addition, the large provision for large amounts of bad debts and impairment of goodwill result in a loss of 1.579 billion yuan in 2020. After excluding the three severely loss-making companies, the total net profit of Zhongguancun NEEQ Companies in 2020 was 8.203 billion yuan, and the average net profit was 9.0242 million yuan (Fig. 1.6).

From the perspective of growth, 424 Zhongguancun NEEQ companies have achieved growth in revenue in 2020, of which 190 (accounting for 20.83%) companies have increased their revenue by more than 30%, and 129 (accounting for 14.14%) have increased it by more than 50%. 433 companies (accounting for 47.48%) have achieved profits for two consecutive years from 2019 to 2020, accounting for 47.48% of the total number of Zhongguancun NEEQ companies, 16 of which have been profitable for two consecutive years with an average net profit of more than 100 million yuan from 2019 to 2020.

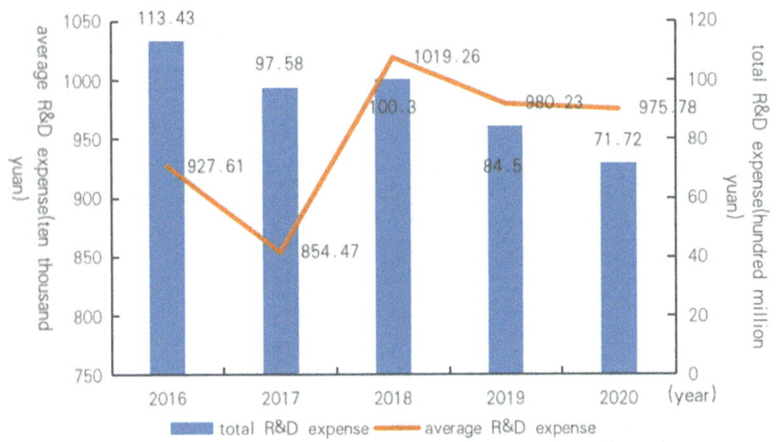

Fig. 1.7 Changes in R&D expense of Zhongguancun NEEQ companies in 2016–2020 (*Source* Wind, compiled by ZLCA)

1.1.6 With a Weak Innovation Vitality, R&D Investment and Output Need to Be Improved

In 2020, a total of 735 Zhongguancun NEEQ companies (accounting for 80.59%) disclosed R&D expenses, which was 7.172 billion yuan, a year-on-year decrease of 15.12%; the average R&D expenses were 9,757,800 yuan, which was basically the same as the 9,802,300 yuan in 2019. 48.16% (354 companies) enterprises have achieved growth in R&D expenses, which is 7.92 percentage points lower than the same period last year; 51.84% (381 companies) enterprises have fallen their R&D expenses year-on-year. From 2019 to 2020, 725 companies that continuously disclosed R&D expenses had a total of 7.084 billion yuan, which was basically the same as last year. From this set of data, the average R&D expenses of Zhongguancun NEEQ companies are the same as the same period last year, and the decline in total R&D expenses is related to the decrease of companies that disclose R&D expenses (Fig. 1.7). In addition, the number of companies with R&D expenses exceeding 100 million yuan is six, which is basically the same as last year.

In 2020, the average R&D intensity of Zhongguancun NEEQ companies was 4.44%, which is basically the same as that in 2019,[9] but it is still higher than the national average R&D intensity of NEEQ enterprises in 2020[10] and the R&D intensity of the whole society[11] International experience shows that more than 10% of R&D intensity is at a relatively high level globally, and such companies are generally considered to have sufficient R&D competitiveness advantages. According to this,

[9] In 2019, the average R&D intensity of Zhongguancun NEEQ Listed Companies was 4.70%.

[10] In 2020, the average R&D intensity of NEEQ companies across the country was 3.38%.

[11] In 2020, the ratio of the country's annual research and development (R&D) expenses to GDP is 2.40%.

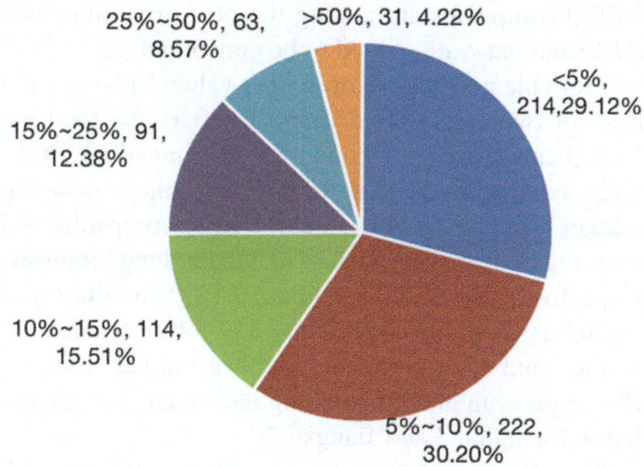

Fig. 1.8 Distribution of R&D intensity of Zhongguancun NEEQ companies in 2020 (*Source* Wind, compiled by ZLCA)

the R&D intensity of Zhongguancun NEEQ enterprises is relatively considerable. 299 enterprises in 2020 were in the list of high R&D intensity enterprises, accounting for 40.68%. However, such proportion has declined, which is a year-on-year decrease of 2.02 percentage points (Fig. 1.8).

From the perspective of R&D output, the reduction in R&D expenses is also reflected in the amount of R&D output. The number of the number of patent authorization by Zhongguancun NEEQ companies in 2020 was 1,282, which was lower than that of 1,450 in 2019. Among them, the number of patent authorization of utility model patents, and design patents were 238, 838, and 206, accounting for 18.56%, 65.37%, and 16.07% respectively. The number of valid invention patents totaled 2,365, a decrease of 3.54% from 2,452 in 2019. Affected by the global spread of the pandemia, PCT patent applications have become more difficult and the process has been more complicated. In 2020, Zhongguancun NEEQ companies filed 11 PCT applications, which was a 56% decrease from 25 in 2019.

1.1.7 Advantages in Regional Comparison Are Obvious, R&D and Innovation Advantages Need to Be Strengthened

This article conducts a comparative analysis of the top five regions[12] in terms of the number of NEEQ listed companies, starting with the core indicators of corporate development such as total market value, revenue, and total assets to analyze the growth of NEEQ companies in the above five regions. Data shows that Zhongguancun

[12] The five regions are Guangdong, Zhongguancun, Jiangsu, Zhejiang, and Shanghai. As of April 30, 2021, the number of NEEQ companies in these five regiones that have announced their annual reports are 981, 912, 853, 619, and 533, respectively.

NEEQ companies are among the best in various indicators, but the advantages of R&D and innovation need to be consolidated.

From the perspective of market value, Zhongguancun and Guangdong have been best for two consecutive years. In 2020, the total market value of Zhongguancun NEEQ enterprises is second only to Guangdong Province, and the number of high-value companies is tied for the first place with Guangdong. In 2020, the total market value of Zhongguancun NEEQ companies is 292.676 billion yuan, and the total regional market values of Guangdong, Jiangsu, Zhejiang, and Shanghai are respectively 304.33 billion yuan, 2.127536 billion yuan (217.764 billion yuan after excluding extreme values), 204.319 billion yuan and 190.18 billion yuan. In terms of the number of companies with a market value of no less than 5 billion yuan, Zhongguancun and Guangdong each have 7 companies, ranking first and Zhejiang has 4, Shanghai 3 and Jiangsu 2.

From the perspective of assets, Zhongguancun's NEEQ companies ranked first in terms of total assets and average total assets. The total assets of Zhongguancun NEEQ companies in 2020 ranked first with 342.753 billion yuan; followed by Jiangsu NEEQ companies with total assets of 311.774 billion yuan; Guangdong, Zhejiang, and Shanghai had total assets of 265.852 billion yuan, 203.908 billion yuan and 180.134 billion yuan respectively. In terms of average total assets, that of Zhongguancun enterprises in 2020 was 376 million yuan, ranking first.

From the perspective of financing, the financing scale of Zhongguancun NEEQ companies is better than that of the other four regions. Specifically, Zhongguancun NEEQ companies stock issuance scale was 5.979 billion yuan, ranking first. The financing scale by Equity Private Placement was 3.805 billion yuan, far ahead of other regions. The corporate bond issuance scale also leaded other regions with 3.65 billion yuan.

From the perspective of the number of talents with high-level education, the number of employees in Zhongguancun NEEQ companies with bachelor's, maaster's and doctoral degrees accounted for nearly half, which is much higher than that in other regions. It means that Zhongguancun NEEQ companies are more capable of attracting highly educated and high-quality talents.

From the perspective of revenue, the total revenue of Zhongguancun NEEQ enterprises is higher than that in other regions. Despite the decline in the scale of revenue in all major regions in 2020, the scale of Zhongguancun NEEQ companies revenue were still rank first, and the decline was the lowest, showing the development strength of Zhongguancun NEEQ companies.

From the perspective of the number of Select companies in each region, the number in Zhongguancun and Jiangsu Province is both 8, which is much higher than the other three regions; in addition, as of June 30st, 2021, the number of Zhongguancun NEEQ companies that have been registered and accepted for Select record is 24, which is higher than 19 in Jiangsu Province and rank first.

From the perspective of innovation capability, the R&D investment of Zhongguancun NEEQ companies is not as good as that of Guangdong Province. Zhongguancun NEEQ companies' R&D investment in 2020 was 7.172 billion yuan, which was lower than Guangdong's 7.521 billion yuan. Its R&D intensity was 4.44%, which was lower than Guangdong's 5.62% and Jiangsu's 4.54%, and only ranked third.

1.1.8 The Proportion of Actual Tax Burden to Revenue Continues to Decline, But It Can Be Better

The actual tax burden of Zhongguancun NEEQ enterprises in 2020 is 5.769 billion yuan. It is 19.16% lower than the 7.137 billion yuan in 2019, which is the largest drop (Fig. 1.9). In addition, the average actual tax burden of Zhongguancun NEEQ enterprises in 2020 has droped slightly, from 6,602,200 yuan in 2019 to 6,326,200 yuan in 2020.

From the perspective of the proportion of the actual tax burden to revenue, it has dropped from 3.77% in 2019 to 3.13% in 2020 in Zhongguancun NEEQ enterprises, which is a decrease of 0.64 percentage points (Table 1.20). However, compared with the other regions', that proportion is relatively high. In general, there is still room for further reduction in the actual tax burden of Zhongguancun NEEQ companies.

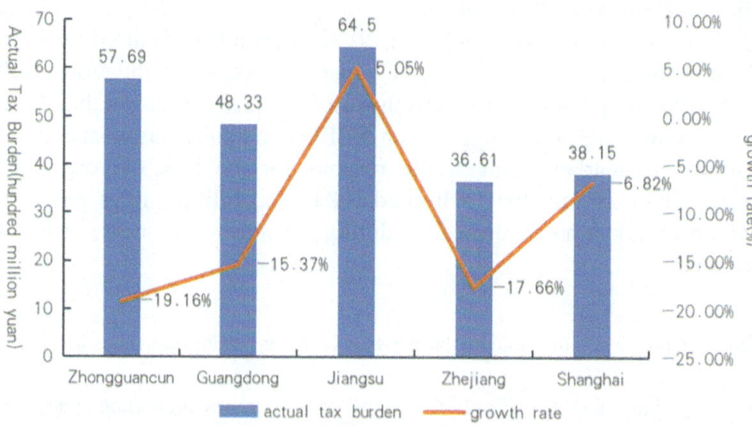

Fig. 1.9 The actual tax burden of the NEEQ companies in each major region in 2020 (*Source* Wind, compiled by ZLCA)

1.2 Zhongguancun NEEQ Companies Development Proposals

1.2.1 Enhance R&D and Innovation Capabilities and Maintain Enterprises Competitiveness

R&D innovation is an important support for an enterprise to build its core competitiveness, and it is also a core driving force for achieving sustainable development. In recent years, Zhongguancun NEEQ companies have been at the forefront of the national NEEQ companies in terms of R&D expenses, but the overall R&D intensity has been decreasing year by year. Data show that its R&D intensity has dropped from 5.55% in 2018 to 4.44% in 2020. At the same time, the proportion of companies that have increased R&D expenses in the number of companies that disclose R&D expenses has also shown a downward trend. From the perspective of the distribution of R&D expenses, the proportion of enterprises with R&D expenses exceeding 100 million yuan among the NEEQ companies in 2020 has increased slightly, but the proportion of enterprises with R&D expenses between 10 and 50 million yuan has slightly decreased. It shows that the COVID-19 has a relatively large impact on companies in the middle of the industry.

In addition, in terms of R&D output, in 2020, the number of patent authorization, of valid invention patents and of Patent Cooperation Treaty applications in Zhongguancun NEEQ companies all declined in various degrees. It shows that the overall R&D innovation ability of Zhongguancun NEEQ companies has weakened.

In addition to market changes, the reasons for the lack of corporate innovation capabilities are related to limited R&D capabilities, long patent review cycles, and insufficient patent protection during the approval process. Therefore it is recommended:

Table 1.20 The proportion of actual tax burden to revenue of NEEQ companies in major regions in 2020

Regions	Revenue		The proportion of actual tax burden to revenue (%)		
	Amount (100 million yuan)	Growth ratio (%)	2020	2019	Growth ratio
Zhongguancun	1840.75	−2.73	3.13	3.77	−16.89
Guangdong	1728.13	6.70	2.80	3.53	−20.68
Jiangsu	1681.71	8.13	3.84	3.95	−2.84
Zhejiang	1665.62	8.21	2.20	2.89	−23.91
Shanghai	1834.38	−25.03	2.08	1.67	24.29

Source Wind, compiled by ZLCA

One is to improve the efficiency of patent examination and approval. (1) It is recommended that the government reduce and optimize the patent approval process and improve the efficiency of patent approval to stimulate the innovation vitality of enterprises. (2) Decentralize the acceptance of application materials to social organizations or other third parties. As a bridge between enterprises and governments, social organizations have natural advantages in serving enterprises and governments. Due to their professionalism, they can provide some guidance to help companies apply, which can shorten the company's approval cycle to a certain extent. Therefore, it is recommended that the Patent Office decentralize the materials for patent application acceptance. A special social organization or a third party can collect and standardize the materials under the condition of confidentiality, so that relevant departments can free up more staff and time to participate in other process to improve efficiency. In fact, as early as 2018, the Korean Intellectual Property Office entrusted independent institutions to conduct the prior search for inventions, utility models, trademarks, and designs through contract outsourcing. To reduce the workload of examiners, they expanded the outsourcing scope of prior art.

The second is to increase the proportion of priority approval of patent applications by SMEs. (1) It is recommended that Zhongguancun Intellectual Property Bureau work with social organizations and third-party agencies to increase policy publicity. (2) A certain percentage is reserved every year for small and medium-sized technological enterprises for patent priority review.

The third is to suggest that the Ministry of Science and Technology strengthen its support for social organizations or science and technology intermediaries agent and broaden the channels for the transformation of intellectual property achievements. SMEs have limited innovation and R&D capabilities, and they are willing to develop further; the Chinese Academy of Sciences, universities, etc. are also major intellectual property owners, so it is necessary to establish a supply–demand relationship between the two parties. In this process, social organizations and technology intermediaries agente act as third parties and can provide both parties with accurate and efficient services. Therefore, it is recommended that the Ministry of Science and Technology coordinate the contact between social organizations and universities and scientific research institutes. It can support and encourage social organizations to lead enterprises into universities and scientific research institutes, conduct on-site inspections and meet the needs of enterprises, which will eliminate intermediate links, and improve docking quality and efficiency of intellectual property rights. The Zhongguancun Listed Companies Association has been committed to helping the Chinese Academy of Sciences in the transformation of intellectual property achievements. In 2020, the association led more than 10 corporate executives into the Institute of Microelectronics of the Chinese Academy of Sciences. This move was highly valued by the leaders of the National Science Foundation. Most companies expressed on the spot that they hope to reach cooperation with the Institute of Microelectronics on certain projects. Both companies and the Chinese Academy of Sciences believe that this is a more efficient and accurate form of promoting the transformation of results, and hope that this model can be sustained and promoted.

1.2.2 Further Intensify Tax and Fee Reduction Efforts to Reduce the Burden on Enterprises

In 2019, the General Office of the Central Committee of the Communist Party of China and the General Office of the State Council issued the "Guiding Opinions on Promoting the Healthy Development of Small and Medium-sized Enterprises". It stated that "it is necessary to reduce the tax burden of SMEs. Clean up and standardize enterprise-related fees and accelerate the promotion of zero administrative fees for local enterprises. Promote substantial tax reductions such as VAT and implement inclusive tax reductions and exemptions for small and micro enterprises and technology start-ups. According to the actual situation, reduce social insurance rates and support SMEs to add employment." During the NPC and CPPCC in 2020, the government work report pointed out to increase tax and fee reductions. The specific measures are "introduce the tax and fee reduction policies that expire before June, including exemption of small, medium and micro enterprise pension, unemployment, and work-related injury insurance, VAT exemption for small-scale taxpayers, service VAT exemption for public transportation, catering and accommodation, tourism and entertainment, culture and sports, reduction and exemption of civil aviation development funds, port construction fees, and the implementation period are all extended to the end of this year" to further reduce Tax burden of SMEs.

The data shows that in 2020 the average actual tax burden of Zhongguancun NEEQ enterprises as a proportion of revenue has dropped significantly, from 3.77% in 2019 to 3.13% in 2020. The reduction in the actual tax burden is conducive to stimulating the production vitality of enterprises, creating value, and realizing regional economic development. However, compared with other regions (2.80% in Guangdong, 2.20% in Jiangsu, 2.08% in Shanghai), the actual tax burden of Zhongguancun NEEQ companies still has room for further reduction.

In addition, there are still 392 (accounting for 42.98%) Zhongguancun NEEQ companies whose actual tax burden accounts for more than 3.13% of their revenue. From the perspective of industry distribution, these 392 companies are dominated by Manufacturing, Information Transmission, Software and IT services. Among them, there are 117 manufacturing companies, accounting for 29.85%. Many of these are manufacturing high-end equipment such as aerospace-related equipment, integrated circuit, and special equipment and instrument. There are 165 companies working on Information transmission, Software and IT services, accounting for 42.09%. Among these companies, there are many high-quality industry companies such as integrated circuit design, data processing and storage services. If the tax burden is too heavy, it is not conducive to the development of enterprises in this type of industry.

Since the actual tax burden of Zhongguancun NEEQ companies account for a relatively high proportion of revenue, as well as the excessive tax burden of some high-end equipment manufacturing and high-quality information technology industry enterprises, it is recommended that the government departments take measures to release certain tax and fee burden and guide the healthy development of Beijing's key high-tech industries such as the new generation of information technology and integration, electrical circuits, medicine and health, intelligent equipment, energy conservation and environmental protection, new energy vehicles, new materials, artificial intelligence, software and information services, and technology services.

1.2.3 Strengthen the Management of Corporate Accounts Receivable and Withdraw Funds in a Timely Manner

Accounts receivable is an important current assets with high risk of an enterprise. The collection of accounts receivable will directly affect the company's cash flow and daily capital operations. If the accounts receivable management mechanism is not sound, the scale is large, and the payment cycle is longer, it will increase the difficulty of collection, increase the possibility of bad debts. In severe cases, it can become the last one factor to crush the enterprise.

In 2020, the overall scale of accounts receivable will decline slightly. The accounts receivable of the 912 Zhongguancun NEEQ companies was 46.452 billion yuan, a year-on-year decrease of 3.12%, which was higher than the 2.73% decrease in total revenue, which means that the debt clearing work has achieved certain results, but still need to pay attention:

First, accounts receivable takes a high percent of revenue. 250 companies (accounting for 27.41%) accounted for not less than 50% of revenue, 240 of which were private enterprises. 71 companies accounted for not less than 100% of revenue, 66 of which are private enterprises.

Second, the turnover days of some enterprises' accounts receivable have increased. The data shows that 29.50% of the companies' accounts receivable turnover days are higher than 180 days and that of 88 companies are higher than 365 days. In addition, the turnover days of 48.90% enterprises increased year-on-year, indicating that it is more difficult for companies to collect payments.

Third, the scale of accounts receivable is large, which seriously occupies the working capital of the enterprise. In 2020, the average size of the accounts receivable of Zhongguancun NEEQ Companies was 50.9342 million yuan, and the accounts receivable of 212 (23.25%) enterprises exceeded this size. There are 101 enterprises with the accounts receivable scale not less than 100 million yuan and 2 with that not less than 1 billion yuan.

While the overall scale of accounts receivable is declining, it is necessary to pay attention to a series of problems that affect business operations, such as the relatively high proportion of accounts receivable in revenue, the increase in accounts receivable turnover days, and the excessive scale of accounts receivable.

Based on the above problems with accounts receivable, on the one hand, it is recommended that companies increase the management and dunning of accounts receivable. On the other hand, the government increase its efforts to clear debts and effectively help companies solve the problem of excessive accounts receivable.

Chapter 2
Report on Profitability of Zhongguancun NEEQ Listed Companies in 2020

2.1 Revenue Situation

2.1.1 Overall Revenue Situation of Zhongguancun NEEQ Listed Companies in 2020

Due to the decrease in the number of listed enterprises and the impact of the COVID-19 epidemic, the total revenue of Zhongguancun NEEQ Listed Companies decreased in 2020, but the overall quality steadily improved. In 2020, the total revenue of Zhongguancun NEEQ Listed Companies was 184.075 billion yuan, down 10.94% year-on-year[1]; the average revenue was 202 million yuan, up 5.76% year-on-year. From the change of Zhongguancun NEEQ Listed Companies' revenue in the past five years, the total revenue reached a peak of 242.148 billion yuan in 2017 as the number of Zhongguancun NEEQ Listed Companies increased, after which the total business revenue declined year by year due to the decrease in the number of enterprises; however, from the perspective of average revenue, the average revenue of Zhongguancun NEEQ Listed Companies in the past five years showed an overall growth trend and the quality of enterprises steadily improved (see Fig. 2.1).

For the first time, the total revenue of going concerns declined due to the impact of the COVID-19 epidemic. The total revenue of the going concerns from 2019 to 2020 was 182.615 billion yuan in 2020, a year-on-year decrease of 2.99%. The decline in the going concerns' revenue was mainly related to the COVID-19 epidemic. In early 2020, the unexpected outbreak and spread of COVID-19 epidemic delayed the resumption of work and production of enterprises, disrupting their original production and operation arrangements. Based on this situation, the government issued a

[1] Three enterprises with huge losses, namely CAPITAL HELICOPTER, CHINAEQUITY and HNA COLD CHAIN, have been excluded.

Zhongguancun Listed Companies Association, *The Growth Report of Zhongguancun NEEQ Listed Companies (2021)*, Current Chinese Economic Report Series,
https://doi.org/10.1007/978-981-19-1242-9_2

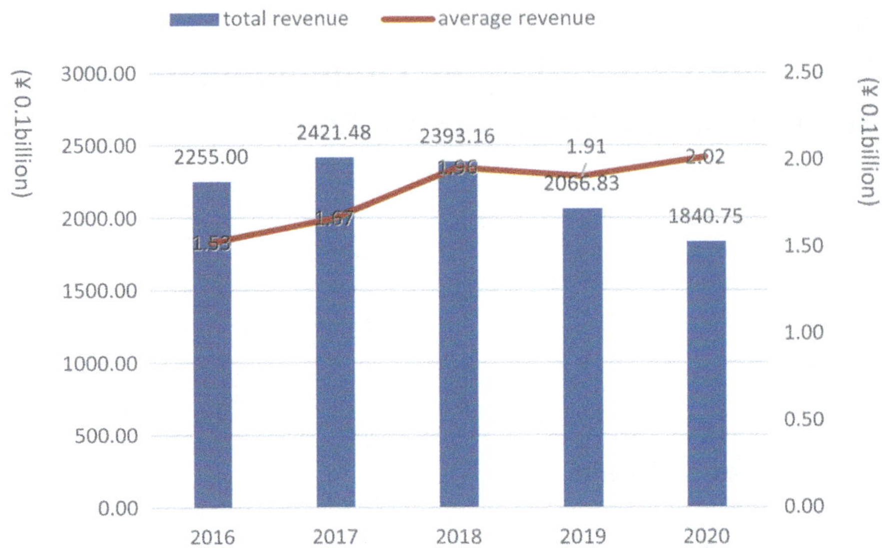

Fig. 2.1 Changes of Zhongguancun NEEQ Listed Companies' total and average revenue from 2016 to 2020. *Source* Wind, compiled by ZLCA

series of tax and fee reduction measures to ease the burden of enterprises and ensure their orderly resumption of production. The series of policies effectively stimulated the vitality of enterprises' production and operation, but the revenue of aggregated consumer service industries, such as wholesale and retail businesses, offline education and training, transportation, catering services, culture, sports and entertainment, and employee-intensive manufacturing industries were still affected.

From the angle of market classification, the average revenue scale of Zhongguancun NEEQ Listed Companies showed a clear decreasing trend from the Select, Innovation to the Base. The total revenue of the seven Zhongguancun NEEQ Listed Companies in the Select was 8.053 billion yuan, accounting for 4.37% of the total revenue of Zhongguancun NEEQ Listed Companies, with an average revenue of 1.150 billion yuan; the total revenue of enterprises in the Innovation was 87.265 billion yuan, accounting for 47.41% of the total revenue of Zhongguancun NEEQ Listed Companies, with an average revenue of 637 million yuan, which was about half of the average revenue of enterprises in the Select. The total revenue of enterprises in the Base was 88.757 billion yuan, accounting for 48.22% of the total revenue of Zhongguancun NEEQ Listed Companies, with an average revenue of 116 million yuan (see Table 2.1).

In terms of growth, nearly half of Zhongguancun NEEQ Listed Companies' revenue achieved positive growth in 2020, and more than 20% of enterprises achieved an increase in revenue of more than 30%. 424 Zhongguancun NEEQ Listed Companies achieved positive growth in revenue in 2020, accounting for 46.49% of the total number of Zhongguancun NEEQ Listed Companies. Among them, 190 (20.83%)

Table 2.1 Distribution of Zhongguancun NEEQ Listed Companies' revenue of different market classifications in 2020

Market classification	Revenue (billion yuan)	Percentage of revenue (%)	Average revenue (million yuan)	Number	Percentage (%)
Select	8.053	4.37	1150	7	0.77
Innovation	87.265	47.41	637	137	15.02
Base	88.757	48.22	116	768	84.21

Source Wind, compiled by ZLCA

Zhongguancun NEEQ Listed Companies recorded an increase in revenue of more than 30% and 129 (14.14%) Zhongguancun NEEQ Listed Companies recorded an increase in revenue of more than 50%. From the angle of market classification, a total of 5 companies in the Select (71.43% of the total number of the Select) achieved positive revenue growth, 71 companies in the Innovation (51.28% of the total number of the Innovation) achieved positive revenue growth and 348 companies in the Base (45.79% of the total number of the Base) achieved positive revenue growth. The revenue growth of enterprises in the Select and Innovation was stronger than that of enterprises in the Base.

From the perspective of industry, Zhongguancun NEEQ Listed Companies were mainly distributed in the Information transmission, Software and IT services and Manufacturing, with the two industries contributing 68.489 billion yuan (37.21% of the total revenue of Zhongguancun NEEQ Listed Companies) and 35.643 billion yuan (19.36% of the total revenue of Zhongguancun NEEQ Listed Companies) in revenue respectively. In terms of average revenue, the Financials enterprises had the largest average revenue scale of 716 million yuan, followed by the Wholesale and Retail businesses with an average revenue of 710 million yuan. The average revenue scale of enterprises in the Information transmission, Software and IT services and Manufacturing mainly distributed by Zhongguancun NEEQ Listed Companies was relatively small, which was 189 million yuan and 177 million yuan respectively, below the overall average of 202 million yuan, (see Tables 2.2 and 2.3).

2.1.2 Distribution of Zhongguancun NEEQ Listed Companies' Revenue Scale in 2020

From the distribution of Zhongguancun NEEQ Listed Companies' revenue scale, nearly half of the enterprises' revenue scale was below 50 million yuan, and the number of Zhongguancun NEEQ Listed Companies with revenue of not less than 200 million yuan accounts for less than 20%. Specifically, a total of 20 Zhongguancun NEEQ Listed Companies with revenue of not less than 1 billion yuan, accounting for 2.19% of the number of enterprises; 35 enterprises with revenue of 500 million

Table 2.2 The top 30 revenue growth rate of Zhongguancun NEEQ Listed Companies in 2020

Ranking	Stock code	IPGP	Market classification	Industry	Revenue in 2019 (million yuan)	Revenue in 2020 (million yuan)	Growth rate (%)
1	871892.NQ	CIVIGAS	Base	Electricity, Heat, Gas and Water production and supply industry	3.2619	724.7119	22,117.74
2	835101.NQ	SMART-SNAPSHOT	Base	Information transmission, Software and IT services	3.1112	99.4496	3096.53
3	837254.NQ	ENERGY	Base	Construction	7.5577	229.8324	2941.03
4	430288.NQ	HONGQI TECHNOLOGY	Base	Information transmission, Software and IT services	0.2057	3.7925	1744.04
5	430731.NQ	KAIDY	Base	Scientific research and technology service	0.0970	1.3381	1279.70
6	832085.NQ	VANGUARD	Base	Information transmission, Software and IT services	18.8746	197.6213	947.02
7	837563.NQ	EXPTECH	Base	Manufacturing	0.1889	1.7634	833.53

(continued)

Table 2.2 (continued)

Ranking	Stock code	IPGP	Market classification	Industry	Revenue in 2019 (million yuan)	Revenue in 2020 (million yuan)	Growth rate (%)
8	835085.NQ	KMY EDUCATION	Base	Education	0.6069	4.8474	698.73
9	430148.NQ	CNGATE	Base	Information transmission, Software and IT services	11.7278	90.5253	671.89
10	430041.NQ	ZJLG	Base	Manufacturing	0.4629	3.3322	619.82
11	430341.NQ	CENTRAN	Base	Information transmission, Software and IT services	28.5611	197.2099	590.48
12	430099.NQ	TPCP	Base	Manufacturing	5.4515	36.9769	578.29
13	430728.NQ	YUNDING	Base	Wholesale and Retail businesses	0.1245	0.8244	562.16
14	430185.NQ	HUAXIN DATA	Base	Manufacturing	0.4717	2.8302	500.00
15	430047.NQ	NORTHLAND	Select	Manufacturing	7.2517	41.4386	471.44
16	837314.NQ	CHINA INTOP	Base	Education	1.4623	7.5965	419.50
17	430292.NQ	VCONTROL	Base	Information transmission, Software and IT services	22.1604	106.1959	379.22

(continued)

Table 2.2 (continued)

Ranking	Stock code	IPGP	Market classification	Industry	Revenue in 2019 (million yuan)	Revenue in 2020 (million yuan)	Growth rate (%)
18	838283.NQ	RETC	Base	Electricity, Heat, Gas and Water production and supply industry	13.7068	63.3453	362.14
19	833044.NQ	HEAVEN-SENT CAPITAL MANAGEMENT	Base	Financials	394.3703	1634.4296	314.44
20	871272.NQ	IDEAL MEDIA	Base	Culture, Sports and Entertainment	7.4825	30.9220	313.26
21	832817.NQ	SHENLINQIJING CULTURE	Base	Information transmission, Software and IT services	4.7114	18.6769	296.42
22	833636.NQ	BANGRUIDA	Base	Manufacturing	2.0149	7.9286	293.50
23	872691.NQ	MUTONG TECHNOLOGY	Base	Information transmission, Software and IT services	0.7893	3.0599	287.67
24	430079.NQ	BEIJING ANPENG	Base	Manufacturing	3.8093	14.5580	282.17
25	832439.NQ	Z+	Base	Leasing and Business services	90.9647	343.1544	277.24
26	836562.NQ	ZHONGTOLIAN	Base	Wholesale and Retail businesses	1.8873	7.0766	274.96

(continued)

Table 2.2 (continued)

Ranking	Stock code	IPGP	Market classification	Industry	Revenue in 2019 (million yuan)	Revenue in 2020 (million yuan)	Growth rate (%)
27	837060.NQ	BX	Base	Information transmission, Software and IT services	11.4386	40.8786	257.37
28	430096.NQ	AIRPURIFIER	Base	Manufacturing	0.8174	2.8599	249.89
29	831632.NQ	JINYIMAO TECHNOLOGY	Base	Culture, Sports and Entertainment	0.3864	1.3348	245.48
30	836468.NQ	PROVA	Base	Manufacturing	27.2526	92.8515	240.71

Source Wind, compiled by ZLCA

Table 2.3 Zhongguancun NEEQ Listed Companies' revenue in different industries in 2020

Industry	Total revenue (million yuan)	Average revenue (million yuan)	Number
Financials	6446	716	9
Wholesale and Retail businesses	36,894	710	52
Transportation, Warehousing and Postal services	1766	252	7
Electricity, Heat, Gas and Water production and supply industry	1228	246	5
Information transmission, Software and IT services	68,489	189	363
Real Estate	554	185	3
Construction	3139	185	17
Leasing and Business services	15,145	182	83
Manufacturing	35,643	177	201
Management of Water Conservancy, Environment and Public Facilities	3625	165	22
Health and Social work	807	161	5
Scientific research and technology service	6161	106	58
Culture, Sports and Entertainment	2730	53	52
Education	1049	46	23
Residential services, Repairs and other services	224	45	5
Agriculture, Forestry, Animal husbandry and Fishery	37	37	1
Mining	125	25	5
Accommodation and Catering industry	12	12	1
Overall	184,075	202	912

Source Wind, compiled by ZLCA

yuan to 1 billion yuan, accounting for 3.84% of the number of enterprises; 103 enterprises with revenue of 200 million to 500 million yuan, accounting for 11.29% of the number of enterprises; 157 enterprises with revenue of 100 million to 200 million yuan, accounting for 17.21% of the number of enterprises; 148 enterprises with revenue of 50 million yuan to 100 million yuan accounted for 16.23%; 449

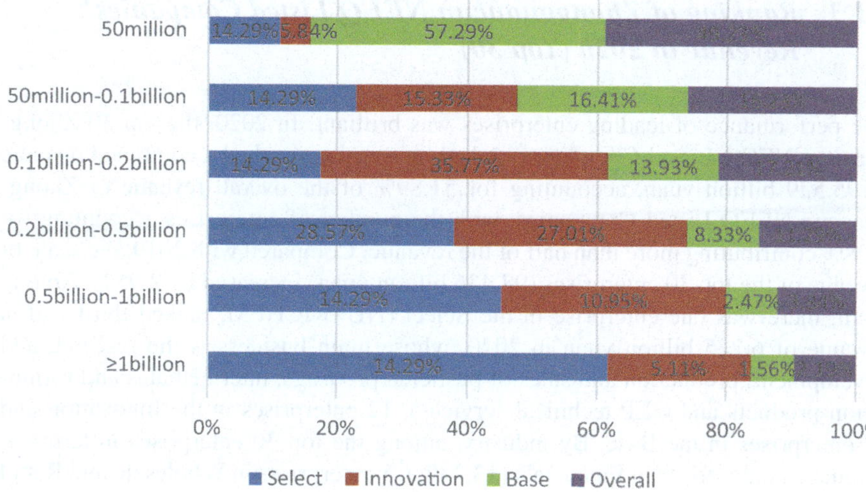

Fig. 2.2 Distribution of Zhongguancun NEEQ Listed Companies' revenue scale in 2020. *Source* Wind, compiled by ZLCA

enterprises with revenue of less than 50 million yuan accounted for 49.23% (see Fig. 2.2).

From the angle of market classification, the distribution of revenue scale of enterprises in market classifications in 2020 showed obvious differences, with the revenue scale of enterprises in the Select mainly concentrated in the range of 200 million yuan or above, the revenue scale of enterprises in the Innovation concentrated in the range of 100 million yuan to 500 million yuan, and the revenue scale of enterprises in the Base concentrated in the range of 50 million yuan or below. Specifically, among the 7 enterprises in the Select, there were one enterprise with revenue scale of over 1 billion yuan, one enterprise in 500 million yuan to 1 billion yuan, one in 100 million yuan to 200 million yuan, one in 50 million yuan to 100 million yuan and one below 50 million yuan (each accounting for 14.29%), and 2 enterprises with revenue scale of 200 million yuan to 500 million yuan (accounting for 28.57%). Among the 137 Zhongguancun NEEQ Listed Companies in the Innovation, 7 enterprises (5.11%) had revenue of not less than 1 billion yuan, and the number of enterprises with revenue scale of 100 million to 200 million yuan, 200 million to 500 million yuan and 500 million to 1 billion yuan were 49, 37 and 15 respectively, accounting for a total of 73.72%, i.e. over 70% of enterprises in the Innovation had revenue scale of 100 million to 1 billion yuan. Meanwhile, 21 enterprises (15.33%) had revenue of 50 million yuan to 100 million yuan; and there were still 8 enterprises (5.84%) with revenue below 50 million yuan. Among the 768 Zhongguancun NEEQ Listed Companies in the Base, only 12 enterprises (1.56%) had revenue scale of 1 billion yuan or above, and most of them (57.29%) had revenue scale of less than 50 million (see Fig. 2.2).

2.1.3 *Ranking of Zhongguancun NEEQ Listed Companies' Revenue in 2020 (Top 30)*

The performance of leading enterprises was brilliant. In 2020, the top 30 Zhongguancun NEEQ Listed Companies ranked by revenue reached a combined revenue of 95.529 billion yuan, accounting for 51.89% of the overall revenue of Zhongguancun NEEQ Listed Companies, with the number of enterprises accounting for 3.28% contributing more than half of the revenue. Compared with 2019, the scale of revenue of the top 30 enterprises (98.436 billion yuan) increased by 2.95%. Among them, there was one enterprise in the Select (NUTRICHEM, ranked third with a revenue of 6.225 billion yuan in 2020, whose main business is the research and development, production and sales of pesticide prodrugs, intermediates and formulation products and GLP technical services), 12 enterprises in the Innovation and 17 enterprises in the Base. By industry, among the top 30 enterprises in terms of revenue, 4 enterprises in Financials (13.33%), 5 enterprises in Wholesale and Retail businesses (16.67%), 6 enterprises in Information transmission, Software and IT services and Leasing and Business services respectively (20.00%) and 9 enterprises in Manufacturing (30.00%).

The revenue benchmark for the top 30 Zhongguancun NEEQ Listed Companies in 2020 was 864 million yuan, down slightly from 939 million yuan in 2019. The top two Zhongguancun NEEQ Listed Companies in terms of revenue scale in 2020 both exceeded 20 billion yuan and were ranked in the top two for three consecutive years, namely HANLINHUI, an IT product sales service provider with a focus on ICT consumer product distribution and retail, enterprise, supply chain and e-commerce services (revenue of 22.518 billion yuan in 2020); and CNBM TECHNOLOGY CO.,LTD, a company mainly engaged in value-added distribution of Huawei and other ICT products, sales of imported network products and sales of medical products (revenue of 20.534 billion yuan in 2020) (see Fig. 2.3).

2.2 Gross Profit Situation

2.2.1 *Overall Situation of Zhongguancun NEEQ Listed Companies' Gross Profit in 2020*

The total gross profit of Zhongguancun NEEQ Listed Companies in 2020 was 37.786 billion yuan, down 18.91% year-on-year; the average gross profit was 41 million yuan, down 4.65% year-on-year. The profitability of Zhongguancun NEEQ Listed Companies declined slightly. From the trend of changes in the past five years, in 2017, the overall gross profit of Zhongguancun NEEQ Listed Companies reached a peak with a total of 62.8 billion yuan, along with the number of enterprises (1,446

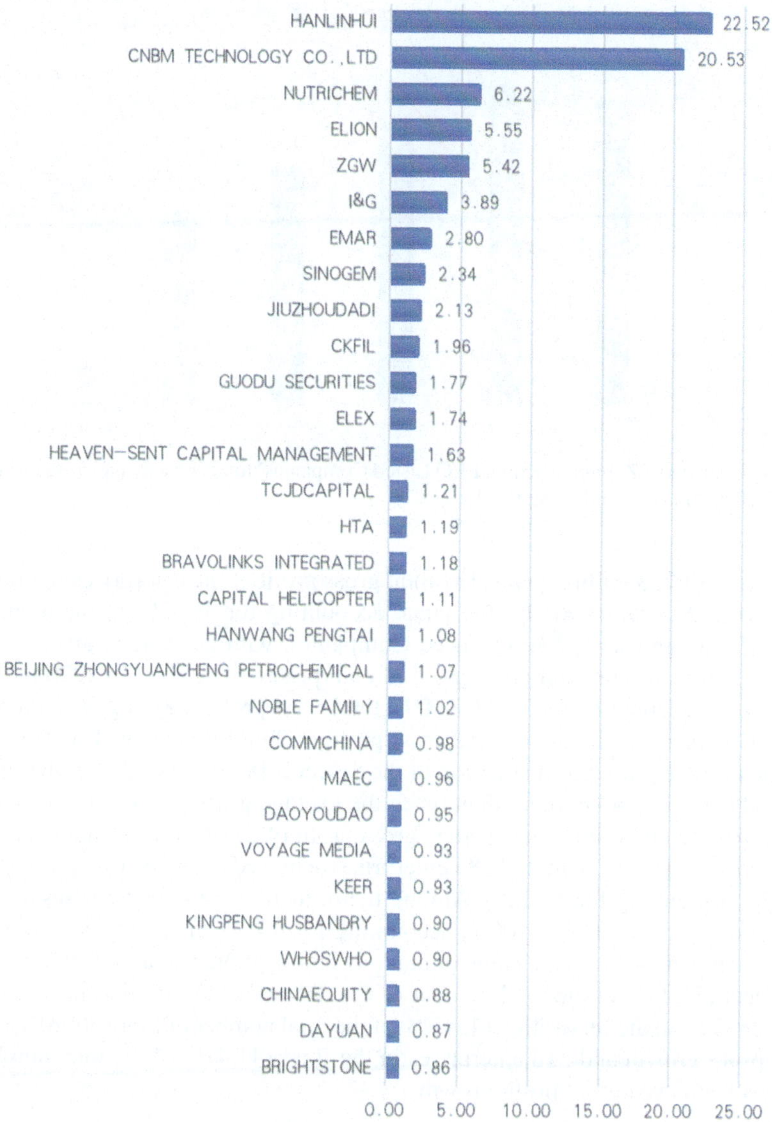

Fig. 2.3 Ranking of Zhongguancun NEEQ Listed Companies' revenue in 2020 (Top 30) (unit: ¥ 1billion). *Source* Wind, compiled by ZLCA

enterprises). The overall gross profit showed a slow decline after reaching a peak in 2018 (47 million yuan), but all remained above 40 million yuan (see Fig. 2.4).

From the angle of market classification, the total gross profit of the seven enterprises in the Select in 2020 was 1.803 billion yuan, accounting for 4.77% of the overall gross margin of Zhongguancun NEEQ Listed Companies, with an average

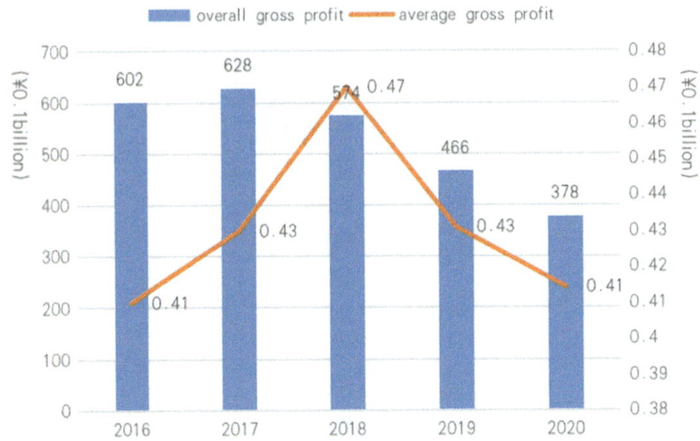

Fig. 2.4 Changes of Zhongguancun NEEQ Listed Companies' total and average gross profit from 2016 to 2020. *Source* Wind, compiled by ZLCA

gross profit of 258 million yuan. The total gross profit of the enterprises in the Innovation in 2020 was 13.961 billion yuan, accounting for 36.95% of the total gross profit of Zhongguancun NEEQ Listed Companies, with an average gross profit of 102 million yuan. The total gross profit of enterprises in the Base in 2020 is 22.022 billion yuan, accounting for 58.28% of the total gross profit of Zhongguancun NEEQ Listed Companies, with an average gross profit of 29 million yuan. The data shows that the average gross profit situation of the Select is far ahead of that of the Innovation and the Base, being more than twice the average gross profit of the Innovation and more than eight times the average gross profit of the Base (see Table 2.4).

In terms of growth, a total of 386 enterprises achieved positive gross profit growth in 2020, accounting for 42.32%. Among them, there were 80 enterprises achieved gross profit growth of over 100%, accounting for 8.77% of Zhongguancun NEEQ Listed Companies. From the angle of market classification, a total of 5 enterprises in the Select (71.43% of the total number of the Select) achieved gross profit growth, 63 enterprises in the Innovation (45.99% of the total number of Innovation) achieved gross profit growth and 318 enterprises in the Base (41.41% of the total number of the Base) achieved gross profit growth.

Table 2.4 Gross profit of Zhongguancun NEEQ Listed Companies of different market classifications in 2020

Market classification	Total gross profit (billion yuan)	Percentage of gross profit (%)	Average gross profit (million yuan)	Number
Select	1.803	4.77	258	7
Innovation	13.961	36.95	102	137
Base	22.022	58.28	29	768

Source Wind, compiled by ZLCA

In terms of industry, except for the Accommodation and Catering industry (only 1 enterprises) whose gross profit was negative, all other industries had positive gross profit. Among them, the Information transmission, Software and IT services had the highest total gross profit of 14.341 billion yuan due to the largest number of enterprises, followed by the Manufacturing with a total gross profit of 10.847 billion yuan. In terms of the average gross profit of the industry, only enterprises in the Financials had an average gross profit of over 100 million yuan (179 million yuan). The second and third highest average gross profit in the industry were in the Electricity, Heat, Gas and Water production and supply industry and the Manufacturing, with an average gross profit of 64 million yuan and 54 million yuan respectively (see Table 2.5).

2.2.2 Ranking of Zhongguancun NEEQ Listed Companies' Gross Profit in 2020 (Top 30)

In 2020, the gross profits of the top 30 Zhongguancun NEEQ Listed Companies ranked a total of 13.702 billion yuan, accounting for 36.26% of the total gross profits of the Zhongguancun NEEQ Listed Companies. Among them, there were three Zhongguancun NEEQ Listed Companies with gross profits above 1 billion yuan, namely CNBM TECHNOLOGY CO., LTD (1.578 billion yuan), a company engaged in value-added distribution of Huawei and other ICT products, sales of imported network products and sales of medical products, NUTRICHEM (1.247 billion yuan), a company engaged in R&D, production, sales and technical services of pesticide intermediates, original pharmaceuticals and preparations, and ELEX (1.060 billion yuan), an international elaborate mobile online game company (see Fig. 2.5).

As for different industries, the top 30 enterprises in terms of gross profit in 2020 were mainly in the Information transmission, Software and IT services and Manufacturing, with 12 enterprises and 9 enterprises in the top 30 respectively, contributing a total gross profit of 4.935 billion yuan (36.02% of the total gross profit of the top 30 enterprises) and 4.532 billion yuan (33.07% of the total gross profit of the top 30 enterprises). Meanwhile, the top 30 gross profit industries also involved Financials, Wholesale and Retail businesses, Leasing and Business services, Scientific research and technology service, Management of Water Conservancy, Environment and Public Facilities, and Electricity, Heat, Gas and Water production and supply industry (Table 2.6).

From the angle of market classification, the top 30 enterprises in terms of gross profit in 2020 were mainly in the Innovation (15 enterprises), with a total gross profit of 6.554 billion yuan (47.10% of the total gross profit of the top 30 enterprises); 14 enterprises in the Base had a total gross profit of 6.001 billion yuan (43.80% of the total gross profit of the top 30 enterprises); and one Select enterprise, NUTRICHEM, had a total gross profit of 1.247 billion yuan (9.10% of the total gross profit of the top 30 enterprises) (see Table 2.7).

Table 2.5 Gross profit of various industries of Zhongguancun NEEQ Listed Companies in 2020

Industry	Total gross profit (million yuan)	Average gross profit (million yuan)	Number
Financials	1609	179	9
Electricity, Heat, Gas and Water production and supply industry	322	64	5
Manufacturing	10,847	54	201
Wholesale and Retail businesses	2539	49	52
Management of Water Conservancy, Environment and Public Facilities	1071	49	22
Health and Social work	242	48	5
Information transmission, Software and IT services	14,341	40	363
Real Estate	107	36	3
Scientific research and technology service	2004	35	58
Construction	508	30	17
Leasing and Business services	2457	30	83
Transportation, Warehousing and Postal services	200	29	7
Education	465	20	23
Culture, Sports and Entertainment	970	19	52
Agriculture, Forestry, Animal husbandry and Fishery	11	11	1
Residential services, Repairs and other services	47	9	5
Mining	47	9	5
Accommodation and Catering industry	−1	−1	1
Overall	37,786	41	912

Source Wind, compiled by ZLCA

2.2.3 *Ranking of Zhongguancun NEEQ Listed Companies' Gross Margin in 2020 (Top 30)*

In 2020, the gross margin of the top 30 Zhongguancun NEEQ Listed Companies was above 80%, with the lowest being 82.04%. Among them, EAGLE INVESTMENT

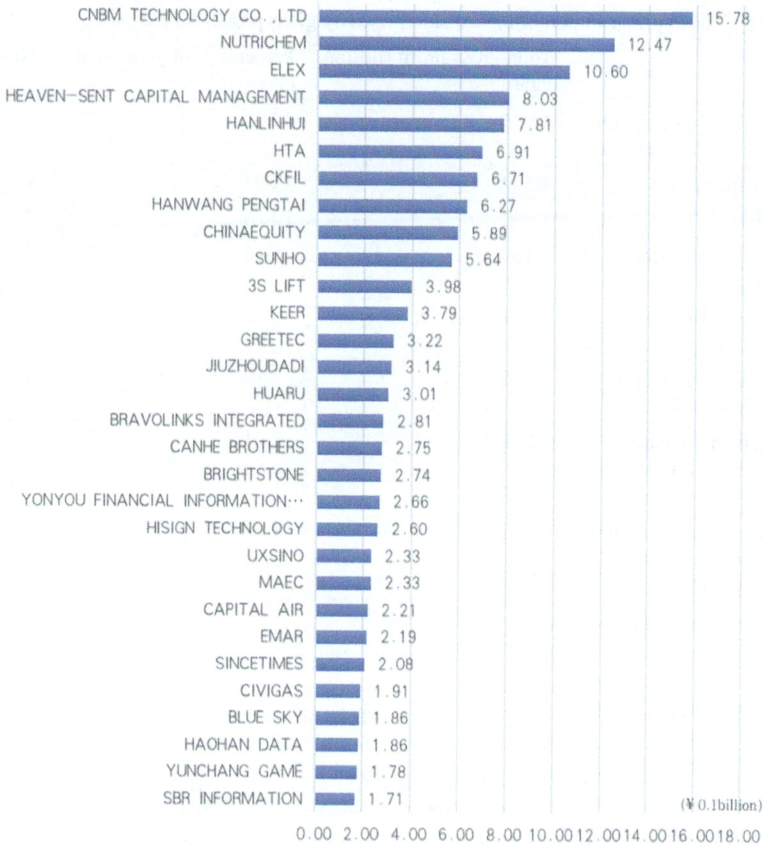

Fig. 2.5 Ranking of Zhongguancun NEEQ Listed Companies' Gross Profit in 2020 (Top 30). *Source* Wind, compiled by ZLCA

HOLDINGS, the Financials industry enterprise; HONSKI and ADS, Culture, Sports and Entertainment industry enterprises; JIANGCHUAN BANKING, the Leasing and Business services industry enterprise, and the Manufacturing enterprise DONGBAOYITONG have no operating costs incurred in 2020, so their gross margins are 100%. In addition to the five enterprises with zero operating costs, the remaining 11 Zhongguancun NEEQ Listed Companies with gross margins above 90%. Meanwhile, there were 30 enterprises with higher gross profit margins, mainly concentrating in the Information transmission, Software and IT services (15), the Manufacturing (4) and the Culture, Sports and Entertainment (4) (see Table 2.8).

Table 2.6 Industry distribution of top 30 enterprises by gross profit in 2020

Industry	Total gross profit (billion yuan)	Percentage of gross profit (%)	Number
Information transmission, Software and IT services	4.935	36.02	12
Manufacturing	4.532	33.07	9
Financials	1.392	10.16	2
Wholesale and Retail businesses	1.159	8.46	2
Leasing and Business services	0.951	6.94	2
Scientific research and technology service	0.322	2.35	1
Management of Water Conservancy, Environment and Public Facilities	0.221	1.61	1
Electricity, Heat, Gas and Water production and supply industry	0.191	1.39	1

Source Wind, compiled by ZLCA

Table 2.7 Market classifications of top 30 enterprises by gross profit in 2020

Market classification	Total gross profit (billion yuan)	Percentage of gross profit (%)	Number
Innovation	6.454	47.10	15
Base	6.001	43.80	14
Select	1.247	9.10	1

Source Wind, compiled by ZLCA

2.3 Net Profit Situation

2.3.1 Overall Situation of Zhongguancun NEEQ Listed Companies' Net Profit in 2020

In 2020, affected by the COVID-19 epidemic and a small number of enterprises with huge losses, the total net profit of Zhongguancun NEEQ Listed Companies fell to 1.541 billion yuan, down 81.06% year-on-year; the average net profit was 1.6897 million yuan, down 77.55% year-on-year. In 2020, the net profit of Zhongguancun NEEQ Listed Companies declined seriously, mainly because three enterprises suffered losses of more than 1 billion yuan each under the influence of COVID-19 and other factors, with a total loss of 6.662 billion yuan. Among them, CAPITAL HELICOPTER (832494.NQ), which provides diversified general

Table 2.8 Ranking of Zhongguancun NEEQ Listed Companies' gross margin in 2020 (top 30)

Rank	Stock code	IPGP	Market classification	Industry	Gross Margin (%)
1	833998.NQ	EAGLE INVESTMENT HOLDINGS	Base	Financials	100.00
2	837699.NQ	HONSKI	Base	Culture, Sports and Entertainment	100.00
3	830871.NQ	ADS	Base	Culture, Sports and Entertainment	100.00
4	834096.NQ	JIANGCHUAN BANKING	Base	Leasing and Business services	100.00
5	430044.NQ	DONGBAOYITONG	Base	Manufacturing	100.00
6	872088.NQ	UNITED MONEY	Base	Financials	99.95
7	834712.NQ	PEARLINPALM	Base	Information transmission, Software and IT services	97.31
8	871958.NQ	NEW RAINBOW	Base	Wholesale and Retail businesses	94.57
9	430032.NQ	KEYTEC	Base	Information transmission, Software and IT services	94.53
10	833575.NQ	HEALTH GUARD	Base	Manufacturing	94.38
11	835352.NQ	QUANT TECH	Base	Information transmission, Software and IT services	93.13
12	834785.NQ	YUNCHANG GAME	Innovation	Information transmission, Software and IT services	92.52
13	872453.NQ	LOONG	Base	Culture, Sports and Entertainment	92.47
14	835785.NQ	PROMISINGKIDS	Base	Information transmission, Software and IT services	90.53
15	430047.NQ	NORTHLAND	Select	Manufacturing	90.48

(continued)

Table 2.8 (continued)

Rank	Stock code	IPGP	Market classification	Industry	Gross Margin (%)
16	834195.NQ	SINCETIMES	Innovation	Information transmission, Software and IT services	90.04
17	836984.NQ	SEMBOO	Base	Scientific research and technology service	89.19
18	873126.NQ	WI-TECH	Base	Information transmission, Software and IT services	88.96
19	430285.NQ	INNOTELE	Base	Information transmission, Software and IT services	88.80
20	835003.NQ	CHINA DRAGON	Innovation	Culture, Sports and Entertainment	86.97
21	838780.NQ	YIQIDANGQIAN	Base	Information transmission, Software and IT services	86.95
22	870000.NQ	LONG DEPOSIT OF SCIENCE AND TECHNOLOGY	Base	Information transmission, Software and IT services	86.79
23	871070.NQ	YINSHANG	Base	Information transmission, Software and IT services	85.16
24	835798.NQ	SEC	Base	Education	84.47
25	837344.NQ	TRI-PRIME GENE	Innovation	Manufacturing	84.00
26	833962.NQ	FOF CAPITAL	Base	Financials	83.87
27	835447.NQ	VIZHUO	Base	Information transmission, Software and IT services	83.23
28	872733.NQ	SILICON VALLEY	Base	Information transmission, Software and IT services	83.05

(continued)

Table 2.8 (continued)

Rank	Stock code	IPGP	Market classification	Industry	Gross Margin (%)
29	832929.NQ	RSC GROUP	Innovation	Information transmission, Software and IT services	82.99
30	430053.NQ	GUOXUE TIMES	Base	Information transmission, Software and IT services	82.04

Source Wind, compiled by ZLCA

aviation services and airport services, had the highest loss of 2.61 billion yuan in 2020 under the major impact of the COVID-19 epidemic and the Group's entry into bankruptcy reorganization proceedings. CHINAEQUITY (833858.NQ), one of the earliest independent institutions engaged in venture capital and private equity investment in China, had the highest loss of 2.61 billion yuan in 2020 due to its holding subsidiary Hifuture (002168.SZ) underwent business transformation and the launch of its game products was delayed, failing to contribute revenue to the company as expected, coupled with the company's provision for goodwill impairment (a total of 1.657 billion yuan) on its holding subsidiaries Hifuture (002168.SZ) and DKM Games (CHENGDU DUOKEMENG NETWORK TECHNOLOGY CO., LTD.), resulting in a higher loss of 2.474 billion yuan. HNA COLD CHAIN (831900.NQ), which is dedicated to warehousing, transportation and distribution services for third-party cold chain logistics, was affected by the COVID-19 epidemic and completely ceased its procurement execution business mainly for cross-border fresh produce. In addition, it made large provisions for bad debts and impairment of goodwill, resulting in a loss of 1.579 billion yuan in 2020. After excluding the three severe loss-making enterprises, the total net profit of Zhongguancun NEEQ Listed Companies in 2020 was 8,203 million yuan, with an average net profit of 90.242 million yuan (see Fig. 2.6).

From the angle of market classification, the net profit situation of Zhongguancun NEEQ Listed Companies in 2020 decreased from the Select, the Innovation to the Base. Specifically, due to the serious losses of the three enterprises mentioned above, the overall enterprises of the Base were in a loss state in 2020, with a loss of 2.306 billion yuan, with an average loss of 3 million yuan per enterprise. After excluding the three enterprises with serious losses, the Zhongguancun NEEQ Listed Companies in the Base achieved a total net profit of 4.356 billion yuan in 2020, with an average net profit of 6 million yuan. The total net profit of enterprises in the Innovation was 3.351 billion yuan, with an average net profit of 24 million yuan, four times that of enterprises in the Base. 7 enterprises in the Select had a total net profit of 495 million yuan, with an average net profit of 71 million yuan, approximately three times the

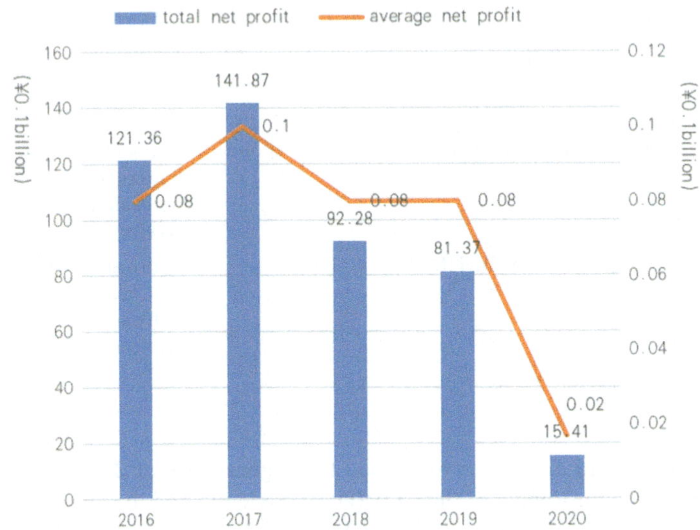

Fig. 2.6 Change in Zhongguancun NEEQ Listed Companies' total and average net profit from 2016 to 2020. *Source* Wind, compiled by ZLCA

Table 2.9 Net Profit of Zhongguancun NEEQ Listed Companies of different market classifications in 2020

Market classification	Total net profit	Average net profit	Number
Select	4.95	0.71	7
Innovation	33.51	0.24	137
Base	−23.06	−0.03	768
Base (adjusted)	43.56	0.06	765

Source Wind, compiled by ZLCA

average net profit of the Innovation and 12 times the average net profit of the Base (see Table 2.9).

2.3.2 *Overall Analysis of Profit and Loss*

From the perspective of the overall profit and loss situation of Zhongguancun NEEQ Listed Companies for the six consecutive years from 2015 to 2020, due to the overall market environment and other factors, the proportion of profitable enterprises to the total number of Zhongguancun NEEQ Listed Companies in that year showed a continuous downward trend, from 76.03% in 2015 to 57.91% in 2019; in 2020, a total of 537 Zhongguancun NEEQ Listed Companies achieved profit, accounting for

Table 2.10 Profit and Loss Statistics of Zhongguancun NEEQ Listed Companies from 2015 to 2020

Year	Number of profitable enterprises	Number of loss-making enterprises	Proportion of profitable enterprises (%)
2015	574	181	76.03
2016	1022	413	71.22
2017	978	468	67.63
2018	734	490	59.97
2019	626	455	57.91
2020	537	375	58.88

Source Wind, compiled by ZLCA

Table 2.11 Profit and Loss Statistics of Zhongguancun NEEQ Listed Companies of different market classifications in 2020

Market classification	Number of profitable enterprises	Number of loss-making enterprises	Proportion of profitable enterprises (%)
Select	6	1	85.71
Innovation	113	24	82.48
Base	418	350	54.43

Source Wind, compiled by ZLCA

58.88%, and the proportion of profitable enterprises rebounded slightly compared to 2019 (see Table 2.10).

From the angle of market classification, the percentage of profitable enterprises in the Select and Innovation (both reaching over 80%) was significantly higher than that of the Base. Only 418 (54.53%) of the Zhongguancun NEEQ Listed Companies in the Base made a profit in 2020, with nearly half of them making a loss; 113 (82.48%) of enterprises in the Innovation made a profit; six (85.71%) of the seven enterprises in the Select made a profit, with only one in deficit (see Table 2.11).

In terms of growth, a total of 433 enterprises achieved profitability for two consecutive years from 2019 to 2020, accounting for 47.48% of the total number of Zhongguancun NEEQ Listed Companies. Among them, a total of 16 enterprises, with a strong profitability, were profitable for two consecutive years and had an average net profit higher than 100 million yuan in 2019 and 2020 (see Table 2.12).

Table 2.12 2019–2020 Zhongguancun NEEQ Listed Companies with two consecutive years of profit and average net profit above 100 million yuan

Number	Stock Code	IPGP	Market classification	Industry	Net profit in 2019	Net profit in 2020	Average net profit from 2019 to 2020
1	430719.NQ	TCJDCAPITAL	Base	Financials	19.48	4.22	11.85
2	834777.NQ	I&G	Base	Leasing and Business services	8.31	8.34	8.32
3	870488.NQ	GUODU SECURITIES	Base	Financials	5.40	8.44	6.92
4	872801.NQ	ELEX	Base	Information transmission, Software and IT services	6.21	5.38	5.79
5	832924.NQ	BRIGHTSTONE	Innovation	Manufacturing	5.67	3.22	4.45
6	833499.NQ	CKFIL	Base	Leasing and Business services	3.80	3.23	3.52
7	834082.NQ	CNBM TECHNOLOGY CO., LTD	Innovation	Information transmission, Software and IT services	2.98	3.32	3.15
8	833819.NQ	NUTRICHEM	Select	Manufacturing	2.67	3.14	2.91
9	833044.NQ	HEAVEN-SENT CAPITAL MANAGEMENT	Base	Financials	1.20	4.05	2.63
10	430005.NQ	HTA	Innovation	Manufacturing	2.79	2.43	2.61
11	835281.NQ	HANLINHUI	Innovation	Wholesale and Retail businesses	2.16	1.86	2.01
12	831344.NQ	3S LIFT	Innovation	Manufacturing	1.42	1.85	1.63
13	834344.NQ	CHINA POST FUND	Base	Financials	1.52	1.46	1.49
14	430277.NQ	SHENGSHANG EDUCATION	Innovation	Leasing and Business services	1.73	0.50	1.12
15	836208.NQ	GREETEC	Innovation	Scientific research and technology service	0.93	1.26	1.09

(continued)

Table 2.12 (continued)

Number	Stock Code	IPGP	Market classification	Industry	Net profit in 2019	Net profit in 2020	Average net profit from 2019 to 2020
16	834003.NQ	WATUER	Base	Information transmission, Software and IT services	1.20	0.85	1.03

Source Wind, compiled by ZLCA

2.3.3 *Distribution of Zhongguancun NEEQ Listed Companies' Net Profit Scale in 2020*

From the distribution of net profit scale, in 2020, about 40% of Zhongguancun NEEQ Listed Companies' net profit scale was in the range of 0–20 million yuan, about 40% of the enterprises were in loss, only less than 20% of the enterprises had net profit of not less than 20 million yuan, and the percentage of Zhongguancun NEEQ Listed Companies with net profit of not less than 100 million yuan was only 1.86%. From the angle of market classification, there was also a significant difference in the concentration distribution scale of net profit among enterprises in different market classifications. As for 768 enterprises in the Base, 349 (45.44%) had net profit of 0–20 million yuan, 350 (45.57%) were in loss, and less than 3% (2.99%) had net profit of 50 million yuan or more. The net profit scale of 137 enterprises in the Innovation in 2020 was mainly concentrated in the range of 20 to 50 million yuan, accounting for 40.15%; 28.47% of the enterprises had net profits of 0–20 million yuan; 13.87% of the enterprises had net profits of 50 million yuan or more; and 17.52% of the enterprises had losses. The net profit scale of 7 enterprises in the Select in 2020 was concentrated in the range of 20 to 80 million yuan, with two enterprises with net profit in the range of 20 to 50 million yuan and 50 to 80 million yuan respectively (28.57% respectively, or 57.14% in total) (see Fig. 2.7).

2.3.4 *Ranking of Zhongguancun NEEQ Listed Companies' Net Profit in 2020 (Top 30)*

In 2020, the total net profit of the top 30 Zhongguancun NEEQ Listed Companies was 6.946 billion yuan, with a net profit threshold of 71 million yuan for enterprises to become the top 30, a slight increase compared to 69 million yuan in 2019. Among them, 17 (56.67%) enterprises had net profits of 100 million yuan or more; three

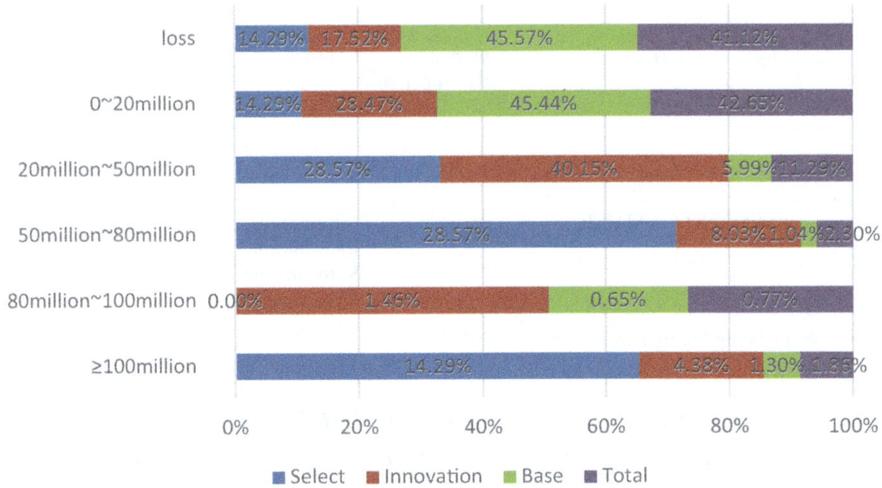

Fig. 2.7 Scale distribution of Zhongguancun NEEQ Listed Companies' net profit in 2020. *Source* Wind, compiled by ZLCA

enterprises had net profits of 500 million yuan or more, namely GUODU SECURITIES, a comprehensive securities company, I&G, a national professional guarantee institution with credit guarantee as its main business, and ELEX, an international boutique mobile game company integrating R&D and operation (see Fig. 2.8).

2.4 ROA and ROE

As mentioned above, due to the three companies in the Base incurring severe losses[2] in 2020, the return on assets (ROA) and return on equity (ROE)[3] of Zhongguancun NEEQ Listed Companies in 2020 were just 0.45% and 0.89% respectively. Excluding these three severe loss-making enterprises, the ROA and ROE of Zhongguancun NEEQ Listed Companies in 2020 were 2.49% and 4.92% respectively. As can be seen, compared to 2019, the ROA decreased slightly and the ROE increased by 0.62% (see Table 2.13).

From the angle of market classification (the comparison benchmark was based on data excluding the three major severe loss-making companies), the ROA and ROE of enterprises in the Select and Innovation among the Zhongguancun NEEQ Listed Companies in 2020 were both much higher than those of the Base. While, the differences between the companies in the Select and Innovation were smaller, with both the ROA at around 4% and the ROE above 7%. Meanwhile, both the ROA and ROE

[2] The three enterprises suffered a total loss of 6.662 billion yuan, accounting for 57.10% of the total loss (11.668 billion yuan) of Zhongguancun NEEQ Listed Companies in 2020.

[3] ROE = net profit/average net assets × 100%; ROA = net profit/average total assets × 100%.

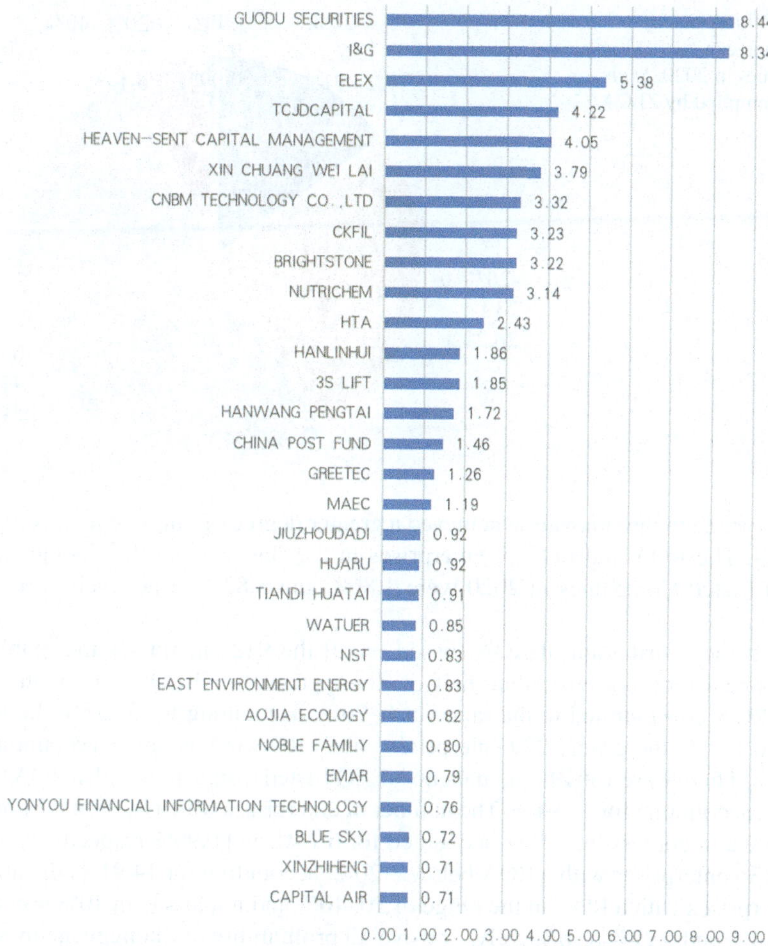

Fig. 2.8 Net profit ranking of Zhongguancun NEEQ Listed Companies in 2020 (top 30) (unit: ¥0.1billion). *Source* Wind, compiled by ZLCA

Table 2.13 ROA and ROE[4] of Zhongguancun NEEQ Listed Companies from 2019 to 2020

Market Classification	ROA (%)		ROE (%)	
	2020	2019	2020	2019
Select	3.51	–	7.32	–
Innovation	4.18	2.78	7.27	4.81
Base	1.86	3.30	3.82	4.26
Overall	2.49	2.66	4.92	4.30

Source Wind, compiled by ZLCA

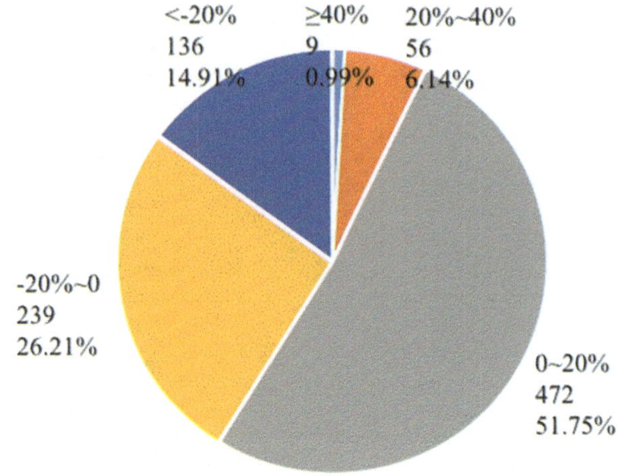

Fig. 2.9 ROA of Zhongguancun NEEQ Listed Companies in 2020. *Source* Wind, compiled by ZLCA

of enterprises in the Innovation achieved a greater degree of improvement compared to 2019. The ROA and ROE of enterprises in the Base among the Zhongguancun NEEQ Listed Companies in 2020 were 1.86% and 3.82% respectively (see Table 2.13).

From the distribution of ROA (based on all the 912 enterprises that published their annual reports), more than half of Zhongguancun NEEQ Listed Companies had a ROA concentrated in the range of 0–20%, accounting for 51.75%. Followed by −20% to 0, there were 239 enterprises with a ROA in this range, accounting for 26.21%. There were 136 Zhongguancun NEEQ Listed Companies with a ROA below −20%, accounting for 14.91%. The number of enterprises with a ROA in the range of 20–40% and not less than 40% accounted for 6.14% and 0.99% respectively. There were 136 enterprises with a ROA below −20%, accounting for 14.91%; the number of enterprises with a ROA in the range of 20–40% and not less than 40% accounted for 6.14% and 0.99% respectively. The overall profitability of Zhongguancun NEEQ Listed Companies should be improved (see Fig. 2.9).

From the distribution of ROE, excluding 29 enterprises with negative average net assets from 2019 to 2020, 531 of the remaining 883 Zhongguancun NEEQ Listed Companies (accounting for 60.14%) had a ROE more than zero in 2020, i.e. their net assets increased. 352 enterprises (39.86%) had a negative ROE, and their net assets lost continuously. Specifically, the ROE of Zhongguancun NEEQ Listed Companies in 2020 was mainly distributed in the range of 0 to 20%, with the number of enterprises in this range totaling 388, accounting for 43.94%. The number of enterprises with a large degree of net assets loss, i.e. a ROE of less than −20%, was 202, accounting for 22.88%; the number of enterprises with a ROE of −20% to 0 was also close to 20% (accounting for 16.99%); however, there were still 16.19% of Zhongguancun NEEQ Listed Companies with a ROE of 20% and above, and 50 enterprises (accounting

[4] Both the ROA and ROE in 2020 are based on the data excluding three serious loss-making enterprises.

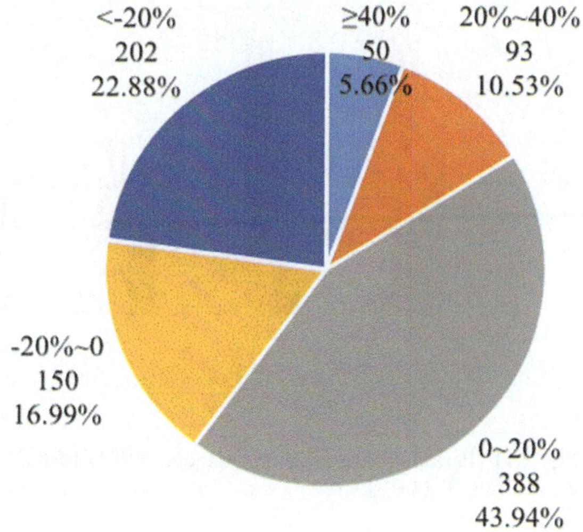

Fig. 2.10 ROE of Zhongguancun NEEQ Listed Companies in 2020. *Source* Wind, compiled by ZLCA

for 5.66%) with a ROE was no less than 40%, and the growth in net assets and profitability of these enterprises were very considerable (see Fig. 2.10).

2.5 Period Charge Situation

In 2020, the total sum of period charge (including selling expenses, administrative expenses and financial expenses) of Zhongguancun NEEQ Listed Companies was 25 billion yuan, down 26.47% year-on-year; the average amount of period charge was 27 million yuan, down 12.90% compared to 31 million yuan in 2019. Specifically, in 2020, the total sum of selling expenses of Zhongguancun NEEQ Listed Companies was 10 billion yuan, with an average selling expense of 11 million yuan, down 8.33% from 12 million yuan in 2019; the total sum of administrative expenses was 13.2 billion yuan, with an average administrative expense of 15 million yuan per enterprise, down 6.25% from 16 million yuan in 2019; the total sum of financial expenses was 1.8 billion yuan, with an average financial expense of 2 million yuan, a 50% decrease compared to 4 million yuan in 2019. Overall, the average selling expenses, administrative expenses and financial expenses of Zhongguancun NEEQ Listed Companies all decreased in 2020 and the decrease in financial expenses was the largest. Looking at the situation in the past five years, both the total selling expenses, administrative expenses, financial expenses and average period charge showed a significant downward trend, indicating that the selling capability, management efficiency and financial utilisation efficiency of Zhongguancun NEEQ Listed Companies have all improved (see Fig. 2.11).

In terms of the composition of period charge, the highest proportion of administrative expenses was 52.48% in 2020, an increase compared to the proportion of 50.88%

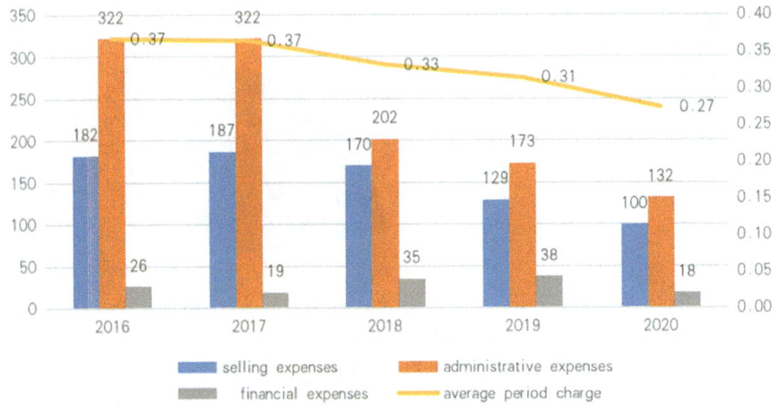

Fig. 2.11 Period charge of Zhongguancun NEEQ Listed Companies from 2016 to 2020. *Source* Wind, compiled by ZLCA

in 2019; the proportion of selling expenses and financial expenses were 39.80% and 7.36% respectively. Looking at the composition of period charge during the last five years, the administrative expenses of the Zhongguancun NEEQ Listed Companies has always been the predominance, but the overall percentage has decreased. The proportion of both selling expenses and financial expenses showed an increasing trend compared to 2016 (see Fig. 2.12).

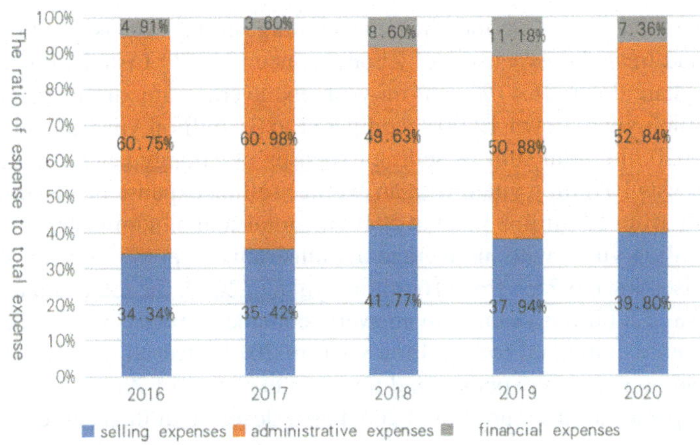

Fig. 2.12 Proportion of Zhongguancun NEEQ Listed Companies' period charge from 2016 to 2020. *Source* Wind, compiled by ZLCA

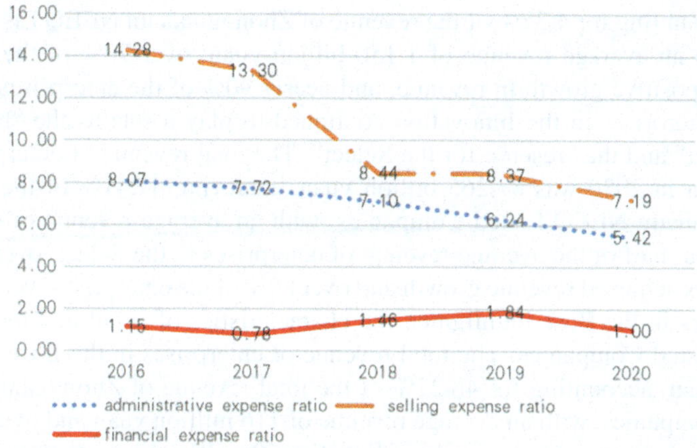

Fig. 2.13 Changes in Zhongguancun NEEQ Listed Companies' period charge ratio from 2016 to 2020. *Source* Wind, compiled by ZLCA

In 2020, the administrative expense ratio,[5] selling expense ratio[6] and financial expense ratio[7] of Zhongguancun NEEQ Listed Companies all decreased compared to 2019. From the trend of the recent five years, the administrative expense ratio and the selling expense ratio decreased year by year, and the financial expense ratio started to decrease after showing an increase in 2018 and 2019, and the financial expense ratio in 2020 (1.00%) was lower than that in 2016 (1.15%) (see Fig. 2.13).

2.6 Summary of the Chapter

The quality of enterprises has steadily improved, with a hierarchical and progressive pattern emerging. Affected by the decrease in the number of enterprises, the total revenue of Zhongguancun NEEQ Listed Companies in 2020 decreased by 10.94% year-on-year, but the average revenue increased by 5.76% year-on-year, nearly half of Zhongguancun NEEQ Listed Companies achieved positive growth in revenue, and over 20% of enterprises increased their revenue by more than 30%. At the same time, a total of 433 Zhongguancun NEEQ Listed Companies have been profitable for two consecutive years from 2019 to 2020, accounting for 47.48% of the total number of Zhongguancun NEEQ Listed Companies, with the quality of enterprises steadily improving. From the angle of market classification, enterprises in the Select had good revenue and net profit, with a clear leadership effect. The total revenue of the seven enterprises in the Select was 8.053 billion

[5] Administrative expense ratio = administrative expense/revenue × 100%.

[6] Selling expense ratio = selling expense/revenue × 100%.

[7] Financial expense ratio = financial expense/revenue × 100%.

yuan, accounting for 4.37% of the revenue of Zhongguancun NEEQ Listed Companies, with an average revenue of 1.150 billion yuan; over 70% of the enterprises achieved positive growth in revenue, and nearly 90% of the enterprises were profitable. Enterprises in the Innovation continued to play a role as the "backbone of the market" and the "reserve for the Select". The total revenue of enterprises in the Innovation in 2020 was 87.265 billion yuan, achieving 47.41% of the revenue of Zhongguancun NEEQ Listed Companies, with an average revenue of 637 million yuan, about half of the average revenue of enterprises in the Select; over half of the enterprises achieved revenue growth and over 80% of the enterprises were profitable. Enterprises in the Base highlighted the characteristics of small and medium-sized NEEQ Listed Companies. The total revenue of enterprises in the Base was 88.757 billion yuan, accounting for 48.22% of the total revenue of Zhongguancun NEEQ Listed Companies, with an average revenue of 116 million yuan and over half of the enterprises having a revenue scale of less than 50 million yuan.

Zhongguancun NEEQ Listed Companies have better expense control and improved quality of operation. In 2020, the total amount of Zhongguancun NEEQ Listed Companies' period charge was 25 billion yuan, down 26.47% year-on-year; the average amount of period charge was 27 million yuan, down 12.90% compared to 31 million yuan in 2019; the average selling expenses decreased by 8.33%, the average administrative expenses decreased by 6.25% and the average financial expenses decreased by 42.50%. The sales capability, management efficiency and financial utilisation efficiency of Zhongguancun NEEQ Listed Companies have all been improved.

The profitability was stable overall, the yield rate of enterprises in the Select and Innovation was significantly higher than that of the Base. In 2020, the ROA and ROE of Zhongguancun NEEQ Listed Companies were 2.49% and 4.92% respectively, with the ROE increasing by approximately 0.6% year-on-year and the ROA decreasing slightly year-on-year, and the overall profitability was relatively stable. Both the ROA and ROE of enterprises in the Select and Innovation were much higher than those of enterprises in the Base, while there was little difference between enterprises in the Select and Innovation.

Chapter 3
Report on Innovation Capability of Zhongguancun NEEQ Listed Companies in 2020

3.1 Innovation Input

3.1.1 R&D Investment of Zhongguancun NEEQ Listed Companies in 2020

3.1.1.1 R&D Expenses

With the severe impact of COVID-19 epidemic in 2020, Zhongguancun NEEQ Listed Companies are facing great challenges and opportunities. Aiming to achieve corner overtaking, it is a critical moment for technology-based companies in particular to seize the opportunity to increase their R&D efforts and consolidate their core competitiveness. But for companies severely affected by the COVID-19 epidemic, realigning R&D strategies in time is a necessary method to preserve their strength. In 2020, 735 Zhongguancun NEEQ Listed Companies, accounting for 80.59% of the total companies, disclosed annual R&D expenses data. The total research and development expenses of these companies reached 7.172 billion yuan, down 15.12% y-o-y. The average R&D expenses were 9.7578 million yuan, basically unchanged from 9.8023 million yuan in 2019. The number of enterprises disclosing R&D expenses decreased by 14.73% compared to 862 in 2019. A specific analysis of the growth in R&D expenses of these 735 enterprises showed that 48.16% (354) enterprises achieved positive growth in R&D expenses, a decrease of 7.92% compared to the same period of last year[1]; the R&D expenses of 51.84% (381) enterprises decreased year-on-year. A total of 7.084 billion yuan was disclosed by the 725 companies that continuously disclosed R&D expenses from 2019 to 2020, essentially unchanged

[1] In 2019, 56.08% of enterprises achieved positive growth in R&D expenses, while 43.92% experienced a year-on-year decline.

Zhongguancun Listed Companies Association, *The Growth Report of Zhongguancun NEEQ Listed Companies (2021)*, Current Chinese Economic Report Series,
https://doi.org/10.1007/978-981-19-1242-9_3

from last year. From this set of data, it is evident that the average R&D expenses of Zhongguancun NEEQ Listed Companies was unchanged from the same period of last year, and the decline in total R&D expenses was related to the decline in the number of enterprises disclosing their R&D expenses. The decline in overall corporate performance had a relatively limited impact on R&D investment (see Fig. 3.1).

The major investors in R&D expenses were not affected by COVID-19 epidemic. In 2020, there was no significant change in the distribution pattern of R&D expenses disclosed by Zhongguancun NEEQ Listed Companies compared with the previous year. There were 6 enterprises with R&D expenses of over 100 million yuan, accounting for 0.82% of the total number of enterprises disclosing R&D expenses; 13 enterprises with R&D expenses of 50 million yuan to 100 million yuan, accounting for 1.77%; 183 enterprises with R&D expenses of 10 million yuan to 50 million yuan, accounting for 24.90%; 164 enterprises with R&D expenses of 5 million yuan to 10 million yuan, accounting for 22.31%; there were 280 enterprises with R&D expenses of 1 million yuan to 5 million yuan, accounting for 38.10%; the number of enterprises with R&D expenses of less than 1 million yuan increased to 89, accounting for 12.11%. In addition, the number of enterprises with R&D expenses of 10 million yuan to 50 million yuan decreased the most, accounting for 24.90% of the total from 26.33% in 2019. The statistical result shows that the impact of COVID-19 epidemic on the R&D investment of the head enterprises of Zhongguancun NEEQ Listed Companies was relatively small and the impact on the middle-tier enterprises was relatively large (see Fig. 3.2).

In 2020, the total R&D investment of the top 30 enterprises reached 2.119 billion yuan, accounting for 29.54% of the total R&D expenses of Zhongguancun NEEQ Listed Companies (see Fig. 3.1). Among them, there are 6 enterprises with R&D expenses of not less than 100 million yuan, which are Internet information

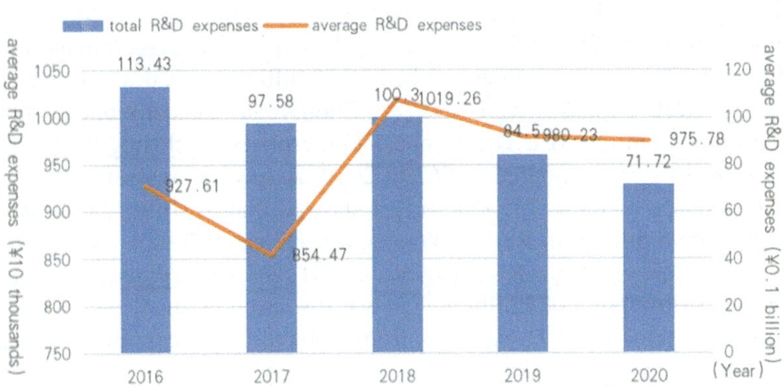

Fig. 3.1 Changes in R&D expenses of Zhongguancun NEEQ Listed Companies from 2016 to 2020. *Source* Wind, compiled by ZLCA

service enterprises called ELEX[2] and SINCETIMES,[3] a chemical pesticide manufacturing enterprise called NUTRICHEM,[4] an information system integration service

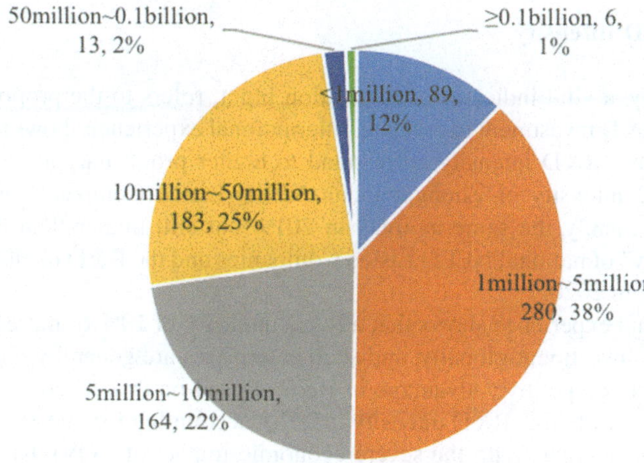

Fig. 3.2 Distribution of R&D expenses of Zhongguancun NEEQ Listed Companies in 2020. *Source* Wind, compiled by ZLCA

[2] ELEX (872801.NQ) is mainly engaged in the development and operation of mobile online games, as well as Internet product services with navigation websites as the core, with 337 game platforms such as Happy Farm and DDTANK. It has developed and operated a series of globally released mobile games such as Happy Farm, Age of Warring Empire, Clash of Queens and Clash of Queens, and has been the agent of Magic Rush: Heroes, Miracle Nikki and other high-quality mobile games.

[3] SINCETIMES (834195.NQ), developed from an Internet game community, has become a diversified comprehensive digital interactive entertainment high-tech enterprise with a collection of mobile games, web games and SNS games. Since 2008, the company has successfully developed and operated QQ Shop, Red Alert War, Undersea World, Empire and Civilization and many other web games with a DAU over one million.

[4] NUTRICHEM (833819.NQ) is an agricultural-chemical products supplier based on R&D and guided by market demand. Its main business is R&D, production and sales of active pesticide, intermediate and preparation products and GLP technical services. At present, the company has formed three categories of more than 100 kinds of high-quality products including a variety of herbicide, fungicide, insecticide, serving for many large global plant protection multinational companies such as ADAMA, Corteva, Nufarm and Lanxess.

enterprise called HISIGN TECHNOLOGY,[5] and software development enterprises called YUNCHANG GAME[6] and HUARU.[7]

3.1.1.2 R&D Intensity

R&D intensity, a vital indicator of innovation input, refers to the proportion of an enterprise's R&D investment to revenue. International experience shows that companies with higher R&D intensity correspond to higher profit margins. In 2020, the average R&D intensity of Zhongguancun NEEQ Listed Companies was 4.44%, which was basically the same as that[8] in 2019, but still higher than the average R&D intensity[9] of national NEEQ Listed Companies and the R&D intensity[10] of the whole society in 2020.

International experience shows that a R&D intensity of 10% or more is at a high level of R&D investment globally, and such enterprises are generally considered to have sufficient competitive advantage in R&D. Based on this criterion, there were 299 enterprises with high R&D intensity in 2020, accounting for 40.68%, a decrease of 2.02% year-on-year. With the severe economic impact of COVID-19 epidemic, the impact on enterprises' R&D intensity is relatively manageable (see Fig. 3.3 and Table 3.1).

---

[5] HISIGN TECHNOLOGY (430021.NQ) specializes in basic technology research, product research and development, information system construction, system integration and technical services with multi biometric recognition technology and intelligent monitoring technology as the core. The company gathers and integrates international leading multi-biometric technologies, including fingerprint, palmprint, face, DNA, handwritten Chinese character handwriting and video license plate, and develops and produces public safety products and solutions with the best performance in China, so as to provide a solid foundation for users to build a more comprehensive social prevention system.

[6] YUNCHANG GAME (834785.NQ) is a company focusing on the development and operation of mobile terminal game products. The company has a strong game research, development and operation capabilities, and the company's products, such as Dragon Tales and Robot Wars, have received enthusiastic response since launched (A-level products).

[7] HUARU (837069.NQ) is committed to military simulation, virtual reality and data application technology research and development and product promotion. In the field of simulation application, such as combat experiment, equipment demonstration, simulation training, joint test, accumulated rich project implementation experience and a series of complete solutions. The company has created domestic leading XSimStudio extensible simulation platform series products with independent intellectual property rights, LORIS joint test and training support platform, data application support platform and a series of simulation application systems in professional fields. The company has passed the national secondary security qualification certification.

[8] In 2019, the average R&D intensity of Zhongguancun Listed Companies was 4.70%.

[9] In 2020, the average R&D intensity of national NEEQ Listed Companies was 3.38%.

[10] In 2020, the ratio of annual research and experimental development (R&D) expenditure to GDP was 2.40%.

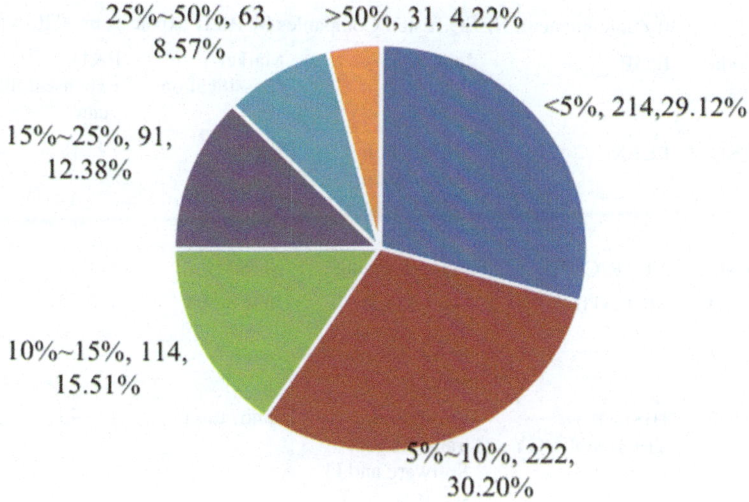

Fig. 3.3 Distribution of R&D intensity of Zhongguancun NEEQ Listed Companies in 2020. *Source* Wind, compiled by ZLCA

3.1.2 Relationship Between R&D Input and Profitability

The stronger the R&D strength of an enterprise, the more irreproducible its products are. The deeper the R&D depth, the more it can enhance the core competitiveness of the enterprise. The data shows that there is a positive correlation between R&D intensity and gross profit margin of Zhongguancun NEEQ Listed Companies, and those with high R&D intensity especially have a higher gross profit margin. Specifically, the average gross margin of enterprises with R&D intensity above 50% reached 71.93% in 2020, an increase of 16.31% over the previous year, which was 5.45 times higher than the average gross margin of enterprises with R&D intensity below 5% of 13.21% in the same year. Because research and development activities can also bring a lot of uncertainty to enterprises, it is important for enterprises to be cautious when making adjustments to their R&D strategy. If the R&D investment is too small, an enterprise will not obtain the long-term competitiveness. Also, a huge R&D investment will result in financial pressure. Therefore, a reasonable R&D intensity in line with the scale, market demand and product characteristics of the company should be pursued (see Fig. 3.4).

Table 3.1 Top 30 Zhongguancun NEEQ Listed Companies by R&D expenses in 2020

Stock Code	IPGP	Industry	Market Classification	R&D Expenses/million yuan
872801.NQ	ELEX	Information transmission, Software and IT services	Base	193.18
833819.NQ	NUTRICHEM	Manufacturing	Select	191.44
834195.NQ	SINCETIMES	Information transmission, Software and IT services	Innovation	155.78
430021.NQ	HISIGN TECHNOLOGY	Information transmission, Software and IT services	Innovation	113.44
834785.NQ	YUNCHANG GAME	Information transmission, Software and IT services	Innovation	103.63
837069.NQ	HUARU	Information transmission, Software and IT services	Base	100.81
839483.NQ	YONYOU FINANCIAL INFORMATION TECHNOLOGY	Information transmission, Software and IT services	Innovation	88.61
430208.NQ	UXSINO	Information transmission, Software and IT services	Innovation	81.90
430010.NQ	MAEC	Manufacturing	Base	79.70
430005.NQ	HTA	Manufacturing	Innovation	67.49
831900.NQ	HNA COLD CHAIN	Transportation, Warehousing and Postal services	Base	64.63
873062.NQ	HANWANG PENGTAI	Manufacturing	Base	60.16
430051.NQ	NSTC	Information transmission, Software and IT services	Innovation	57.23
833858.NQ	CHINAEQUITY	Financials	Base	57.05

(continued)

Table 3.1 (continued)

Stock Code	IPGP	Industry	Market Classification	R&D Expenses/million yuan
833175.NQ	HAOHAN DATA	Information transmission, Software and IT services	Base	54.81
870790.NQ	BLUE SKY	Manufacturing	Base	52.69
430046.NQ	SBR INFORMATION	Information transmission, Software and IT services	Innovation	52.05
834082.NQ	CNBM TECHNOLOGY CO.,LTD	Information transmission, Software and IT services	Innovation	51.10
430052.NQ	CANHE BROTHERS	Information transmission, Software and IT services	Base	51.03
832646.NQ	COMMCHINA	Information transmission, Software and IT services	Innovation	45.46
870840.NQ	ASDC	Information transmission, Software and IT services	Base	43.32
430017.NQ	SUNHO	Manufacturing	Innovation	42.42
833526.NQ	BFUS	Construction	Base	41.90
430330.NQ	ICPC	Information transmission, Software and IT services	Innovation	41.06
836036.NQ	EASTFAIR	Information transmission, Software and IT services	Innovation	41.05
832924.NQ	BRIGHTSTONE	Manufacturing	Innovation	40.64
836346.NQ	EMAR	Information transmission, Software and IT services	Innovation	39.37

(continued)

Table 3.1 (continued)

Stock Code	IPGP	Industry	Market Classification	R&D Expenses/million yuan
430341.NQ	CENTRAN	Information transmission, Software and IT services	Base	36.50
839885.NQ	GAMELEY	Information transmission, Software and IT services	Base	35.53
834046.NQ	JRUION	Information transmission, Software and IT services	Base	35.25
Total				2119.23

Source Wind, compiled by ZLCA

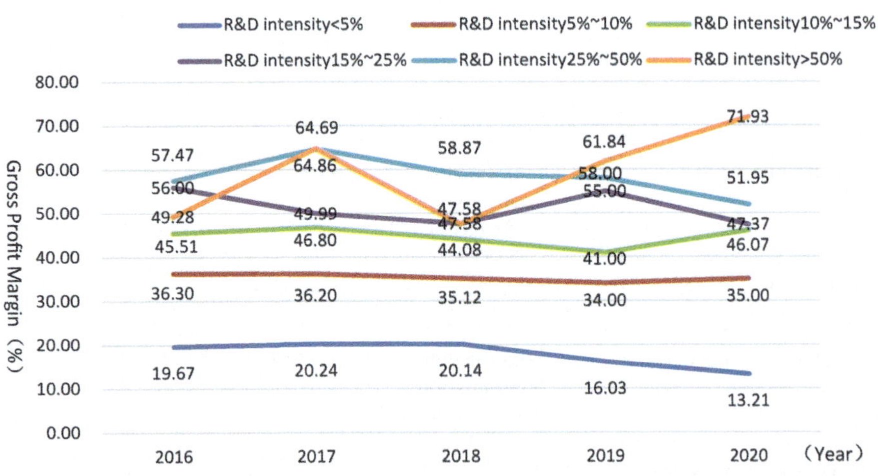

Fig. 3.4 Relationship between R&D intensity and gross margin of Zhongguancun NEEQ Listed Companies from 2016 to 2020. *Source* Wind, compiled by ZLCA

3.2 Innovation Output

3.2.1 Number of Patent Authorization and Ranking

The principles of patent authorization are that the patent is novel, inventive and useful. Once authorized, the patent is protected by laws and becomes the private property of the enterprise. The number of patent authorization is one of the main indicators to measure the capacity, level and quality of an enterprise's innovation output. The higher the number of patents authorized, the stronger the overall strength of an enterprise's innovation output. Among the 1,073 Zhongguancun NEEQ Listed Companies in 2020, the number of enterprises with patent authorization was 355, accounting for 33.08%, and the total number of patent authorization was 1,282, down from 1,450 in 2019. Among them, the number of invention patent was 238, the number of utility model patent was 838, the number of design patent was 206, accounting for 18.56%, 65.37% and 16.07% respectively. The decline in the overall number of patent application in 2020 was inextricably linked to the contraction of some enterprises' R&D investment, and the longer time for the patent application and authorization than that in previous years was also a factor affecting the total decline. In addition, utility model patents continued to be the main force of patent authorization. The listed companies in Zhongguancun, as the main force of science and technology innovation, are supposed to make efforts to increase the proportion of invention patents, which will still be an important direction in the future.

In order to further increase the R&D efforts in the manufacturing industry, the Ministry of Finance and the State Taxation Administration issued the Announcement on Further Improving the Policy on Pre-tax Deduction of R&D Expenses. The announcement states that the actual R&D expenses incurred by manufacturing enterprises in carrying out R&D activities, which do not form intangible assets and are included in the current profit and loss, on the basis of the actual deduction as stipulated, shall be further deducted pre-tax at 100% of the actual basis accounting from January 1, 2021 onwards. If intangible assets are formed, they shall be amortized pre-tax at 200% of the cost of the intangible assets from January 1, 2021 onwards. It means that the additional deduction proportion of R&D expenses for Chinese manufacturing enterprises has increased from 175 to 200%, boosting the innovation capability of Chinese manufacturing industry. It is believed that the overall patent approval in 2021 will also have a good performance (see Fig. 3.5).

In terms of the number of patent authorization, the top 10 enterprises of Zhongguancun NEEQ Listed Companies obtained a total of 249 patents in 2020, accounting for 19.42% of the total number of patent authorization, down 31.50% compared to 363 in 2019, mainly due to the delisting of IAT in 2019, which owned 222 authorized patents. As for the industry distribution of the top 10 enterprises in terms of the number of patent authorization, half of the enterprises (5) are manufacturing; two are information transmission, software and IT services; one each for management of water conservancy, environment and public facilities, construction and scientific research and technology service. The top-ranked company, 3S LIFT,[11] with 62 patents authorized, has 62 patents, belonging to the manufacturing industry (see Table 3.2).

[11] 3S LIFT (605305. SH) is a leading provider of high-altitude security operation equipment and high-altitude security operation service solutions in China. It focuses on the field of high-altitude security operation and is committed to providing customers with an overall high-altitude operation solution of "safe use, simple operation and professional manufacturing". At this stage, the company mainly focuses on the field of wind power generation. The company has core technical advantages in the fields of high-altitude security lifting equipment and high-altitude security protection equipment.

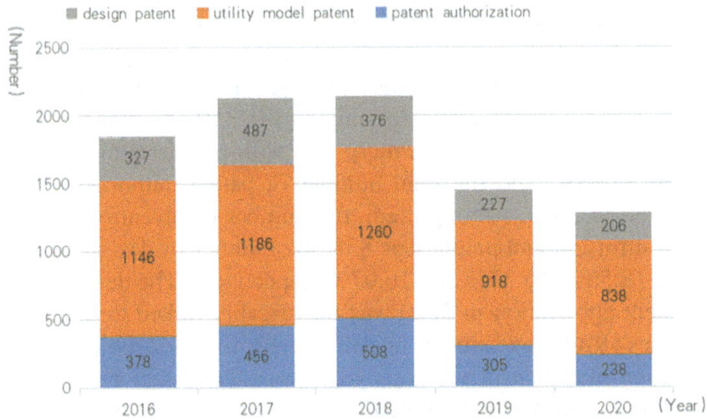

Fig. 3.5 The number of patent authorization of Zhongguancun NEEQ Listed Companies from 2016 to 2020. *Source* Zhongguancun Intellectual Property Promotion Bureau, compiled by ZLCA

3.2.2 Number of Valid Invention Patent and Ranking

A valid invention patent is one that remains valid after a patent application has been authorized. The longer an invention patent is maintained, the longer it takes to create economic benefits. Data shows that only 40% of domestic invention patents have been maintained for more than 10 years, while the percentage of foreign invention patents maintained for more than 10 years is as high as 82.2%. In other words, the average maintenance time of domestic invention patents is lower than that of international invention patents, reflecting that the characteristics of domestic enterprises' innovation output are less investment, short cycle and quick effect. As at December 31, 2020, there were 355 Zhongguancun NEEQ Listed Companies with a total of 2,365 valid invention patents, representing a year-on-year decrease of 4.13%. The trend in recent years shows a slow decline in the number of valid invention patents for Zhongguancun enterprises (see Fig. 3.6).

In 2020, the top 10 enterprises of Zhongguancun NEEQ Listed Companies had a total of 568 valid invention patents, accounting for 24.01% of the overall valid invention patents of Zhongguancun NEEQ Listed Companies, down slightly from 588 valid invention patents owned by the top 10 enterprises in 2019. PIXEL SOFTWARE TECHNOLOGY[12] ranked first for two consecutive years, with an increase

At present, it has achieved the full coverage of the top 20 wind turbine manufacturers and five power groups in China.

[12] PIXEL SOFTWARE TECHNOLOGY (836333.NQ) is mainly engaged in game software development, the company's main products for client games and mobile games. Since its establishment, the company has planned and developed a number of popular Online games such as Blade & Sword, Blade & Sword Online, Zentia, Blade&Sword II and Revenant Adventure.

Table 3.2 Top 10 Zhongguancun NEEQ Listed Companies by the number of patent authorization

Ranking	Stock Code	IPGP	Market Classification	Industry	Number of patent authorizations in 2020			
					Invention patent	Utility model patent	Design patent	Total
1	831344.OC	3S LIFT	Innovation	Manufacturing	1	60	1	62
2	836263.OC	ZHTD	Select	Management of Water Conservancy, Environment and Public Facilities	1	33	0	34
3	836333.OC	PIXEL SOFTWARE TECHNOLOGY	Base	Information transmission, Software and IT services	26	0	0	26
4	835990.OC	SUIRUI	Innovation	Information transmission, Software and IT services	5	2	18	25
5	871848.OC	GREEN JINGHUA	Base	Construction	0	20	0	20
6	870475.OC	BHT ENVIRON	Base	Scientific research and technology service	0	18	0	18
7	832987.OC	PAFER	Base	Manufacturing	0	17	0	17
8	832004.OC	HAILIN AUTOMATION	Base	Manufacturing	0	3	13	16
9	839386.OC	YOOKNET	Base	Manufacturing	0	0	16	16
10	838091.OC	KLT ELECTRIKLT ELECTRIC CO.,LTD	Base	Manufacturing	0	15	0	15
Total					33	168	48	249

Source Zhongguancun Intellectual Property Promotion Bureau, compiled by ZLCA

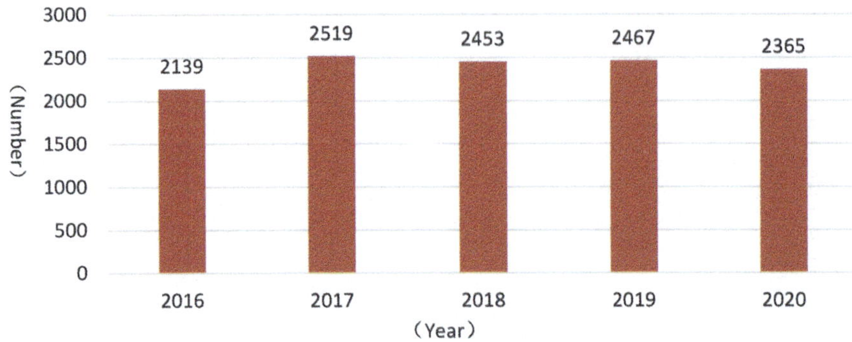

Fig. 3.6 The number of valid invention patent of Zhongguancun NEEQ Listed Companies from 2016 to 2020. *Source* Zhongguancun Intellectual Property Promotion Bureau, compiled by ZLCA

of 26 cases compared to last year, and enterprises such as CPT,[13] RAYSPOWER[14] and NUTRICHEM remained top 10 for two consecutive years (see Table 3.3).

3.2.3 *Number of Patent Cooperation Treaty (PCT)*

Patent Cooperation Treaty, abbreviated as PCT, is an international cooperation treaty in the field of patents, aiming to simplify the process of invention patent protection application in multiple countries and to make the process more economical and effective. Most of the enterprises applying for PCT in 2020 are bio-pharmaceutical manufacturing enterprises, indicating that such enterprises have a strong demand for finding their way to the world and being recognized by the international market.

In 2020, due to the impact of COVID-19 epidemic, which made it more difficult and time-consuming for enterprises to patent application, the number of PCT application of Zhongguancun NEEQ Listed Companies was 11, compared to 25 in 2019, a decrease of 56% (see Fig. 3.7).

Only 6 enterprises applied for PCT in 2020, down 5 from 11 in 2019. All these 6 enterprises were manufacturing industry. In terms of the angle of market classification, there was one in the Select, two in the Innovation and three in the Base. The

[13] CPT (833429. NQ) is the first high-tech enterprise in China that integrates R&D, production and sales of sports nutrition food and provides sports nutrition technology services. For a long time, it has provided safe and effective series of sports nutrition food and professional technology consulting services for national professional athletes and mass fitness people. After nearly a decade of rapid development, CPT's market share is firmly at the top of its industry in China.

[14] RAYSPOWER (430065.NQ) focuses on solar power generation and comprehensive utilization of photothermal innovation. As a state-level high-tech enterprise in the field of new energy, RAYSPOWER has participated in the project approval, design, construction and operation of a number of state-level large-scale solar power stations, such as Golden Sun and BIPV.

Table 3.3 Top 10 Zhongguancun NEEQ Listed Companies by the number of valid invention patent

Ranking	Stock Code	IPGP	Industry	Market Classification	Number of valid invention patent
1	836333.NQ	PIXEL SOFTWARE TECHNOLOGY	Information transmission, Software and IT services	Base	127
2	833429.NQ	CPT	Manufacturing	Innovation	91
3	430065.NQ	RAYSPOWER	Manufacturing	Base	74
4	833819.NQ	NUTRICHEM	Manufacturing	Select	55
5	873062.NQ	HANWANG PENGTAI	Manufacturing	Base	54
6	837344.NQ	TRI-PRIME GENE	Manufacturing	Innovation	45
7	430666.NQ	LVSAN CHEMICAL	Manufacturing	Base	36
8	873530.NQ	BAINENG YINGTIAN	Information transmission, Software and IT services	Base	32
9	835579.NQ	MTD	Manufacturing	Base	28
10	430010.NQ	MAEC	Manufacturing	Base	26

Source Zhongguancun Intellectual Property Promotion Bureau, compiled by ZLCA

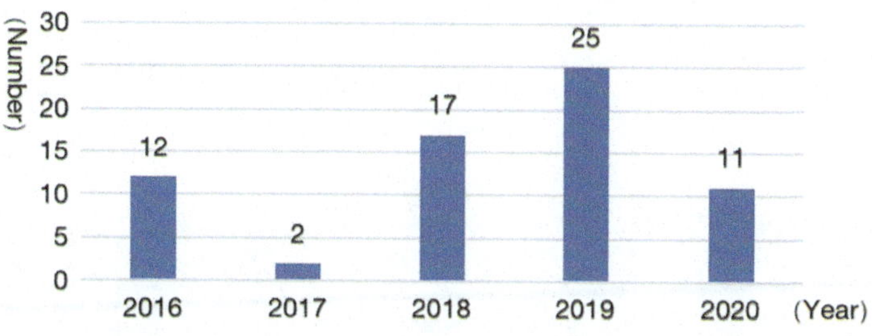

Fig. 3.7 The number of PCT application of Zhongguancun NEEQ Listed Companies from 2016 to 2020. *Source* Zhongguancun Intellectual Property Promotion Bureau, compiled by ZLCA

Table 3.4 List of PCT application of Zhongguancun NEEQ Listed Companies in 2020

Number	Stock Code	IPGP	Industry	Market Classification	Number of PCT applications
1	831344.NQ	3S LIFT	Manufacturing	Innovation	5
2	834367.NQ	MOKOBIO	Manufacturing	Base	2
3	430005.NQ	HTA	Manufacturing	Innovation	1
4	430145.NQ	SUNNY MEDICAL	Manufacturing	Base	1
5	430047.NQ	NORTHLAND	Manufacturing	Select	1
6	870880.NQ	TONGDY	Manufacturing	Base	1

Source Zhongguancun Intellectual Property Promotion Bureau, compiled by ZLCA

outstanding enterprises were 3S LIFT with 5 PCT applications, MOKOBIO[15] with 2 and all other companies with 1 each (see Table 3.4).

[15] MOKOBIO (834367.NQ) focuses on the independent research, development and innovation of in vitro diagnostic technology, and has formed three series of immune platform diagnostic reagents, gene platform diagnostic reagents and related testing services, testing equipment. The diagnostic reagents of the immune platform include four routine general examinations of gastric function and gastric cancer screening products, routine monitoring products of bacterial and viral infection, and maternal and child health care system detection products. Gene platform diagnosis includes nucleic acid pretreatment series reagents, multiple fluorescent quantitative detection reagents, high-throughput gene detection system detection reagents and services; detection equipment includes Mokosensor-A300 colloidal gold immuno-analyzer, Mokosensor C-100 biochemical analyzer.

Chapter 4
Report on Solvency and Operating Capability of Zhongguancun NEEQ Listed Companies in 2020

4.1 Analysis of Zhongguancun NEEQ Listed Companies' Solvency in 2020

4.1.1 Solvency

Solvency reflects the capability of an enterprise to pay its liabilities. Although not directly linked to the growth of corporate profits, it is an important capability to ensure the survival and development of the enterprise, also an inevitable requirement to measure an enterprise's growth. In particular, for the majority of NEEQ Listed Companies in the start-up and growth stages, they need sufficient capital to support their rapid growth, along with a high level of financial risk. Without adequate knowledge of their solvency, NEEQ Listed Companies are prone to cause fund misapplication, which may result in their inability to repay their due debts, the increase of financing costs and higher financial expense ratios and reducing their profitability. Therefore, the report intends to reflect the financial status of Zhongguancun NEEQ Listed Companies through the analysis of their overall solvency, so as to provide reference for enterprises to adjust their own capital structure and rationally plan the proportion of liabilities and financing; and provide a policy basis for relevant government departments to prevent the systematic risk of enterprise operation.

From the perspective of the financial analysis system, solvency is often divided into short-term solvency and long-term solvency. The short-term solvency focuses on the capability to repay current liabilities, while long-term solvency focuses on the capital structure and the capability to repay long-term maturing debts. For short-term solvency, the report uses vital indicators such as current ratio, quick ratio and cash ratio for analysis; for long-term solvency, it uses the asset-liability ratio and cash flow liability ratio for analysis. Through the calculation and analysis of these indicators, it is hoped to obtain a visual representation of the overall level of Zhongguancun

Zhongguancun Listed Companies Association, *The Growth Report of Zhongguancun NEEQ Listed Companies (2021)*, Current Chinese Economic Report Series,
https://doi.org/10.1007/978-981-19-1242-9_4

NEEQ Listed Companies' solvency, so as to provide suggestions for the sustainable and healthy growth of Zhongguancun NEEQ Listed Companies.

4.1.2 Analysis of Zhongguancun NEEQ Listed Companies' Long-Term Solvency in 2020

1. Analysis of Zhongguancun NEEQ Listed Companies' Capital Structure in 2020

(1) Total Assets of Zhongguancun NEEQ Listed Companies in 2020

As at December 31st, 2020, the total assets of Zhongguancun NEEQ Listed Companies were 342.753 billion yuan, a decrease of 6.92% from 2019 (368.225 billion yuan). Among them, the total assets of the enterprises in the Select were 14.661 billion yuan, accounting for 4.28%; the total assets of the enterprises in the Innovation were 84.700 billion yuan, accounting for 24.71%; and the total assets of the enterprises in the Base were 243.392 billion yuan, accounting for 71.01%. The average total assets of Zhongguancun NEEQ Listed Companies were 376 million yuan, of which the average total assets of both the Select and Innovation enterprises were higher than this value, at 2094 million yuan and 618 million yuan respectively, while the average total assets of enterprises in the Base were lower than the average, at 317 million yuan. Overall, the average total assets of the Select were higher, and better than those of the Innovation and Base (see Table 4.1).

Among all Zhongguancun NEEQ Listed Companies, there were 499 enterprises with assets scale of 0–100 million yuan in 2020, accounting for 54.71%, and their total assets scale was 19,244 million yuan in total, accounting for 5.61% of the total assets scale of all Zhongguancun NEEQ Listed Companies; there were 383 enterprises with assets scale of 100 million yuan to 1 billion yuan, accounting for 42.00%, and their total asset scale was 111.574 billion yuan, accounting for 32.55% of Zhongguancun NEEQ Listed Companies' total assets scale; there were 24 enterprises with assets scale of 1 billion yuan to 10 billion yuan, accounting for 2.63%, and their total assets scale was 61.195 billion yuan, accounting for 17.85% of Zhongguancun NEEQ Listed Companies' total assets scale; there were only 6 enterprises with assets

Table 4.1 Total assets of Zhongguancun NEEQ Listed Companies' in different market classification in 2020

Market classification	Total assets (billion yuan)	Proportion of total assets (%)	Average total assets (million yuan)
Select	14.661	4.28	2094
Innovation	84.700	24.71	618
Base	243.392	71.01	317
Total	342.753	100.00	376

Source Wind, compiled by ZLCA

scale of 10 billion yuan and above, but their total assets scale reached 150.740 billion yuan, accounting for 43.98% of the total. The above data shows that there is a clear polarization of Zhongguancun NEEQ Listed Companies' total assets scale, and that the Zhongguancun NEEQ Listed Companies contains a wide range of enterprises of different sizes.

In 2020, the entry benchmark for the top 30 Zhongguancun NEEQ Listed Companies ranking in terms of total assets was 1.122 billion yuan, down from 1.173 billion yuan in 2019 (see Fig. 4.1). Among the top 30, there was only one enterprise in the Select, 13 in the Innovation and 16 in the Base. By industry, of these 30 companies,

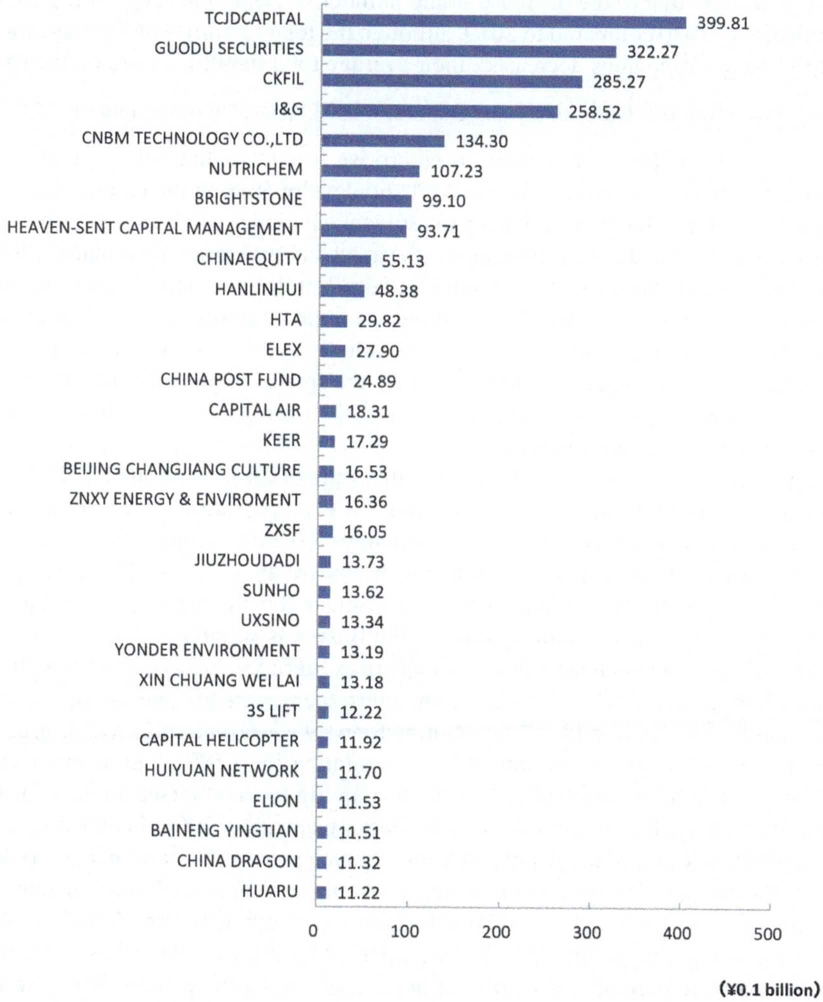

Fig. 4.1 Top 30 of Zhongguancun NEEQ Listed Companies' total assets in 2020. *Source* Wind, compiled by ZLCA

8 were Manufacturing, 7 were Information transmission, Software and IT services, 5 were Financials and 10 were other industries in total.

(2) Total Liabilities of Zhongguancun NEEQ Listed Companies in 2020

As at December 31st, 2020, the total liabilities of Zhongguancun NEEQ Listed Companies were 165.957 billion yuan, a year-on-year decrease of 7.58%. Among them, the total liabilities of the Select, Innovation and Base were 6.812 billion yuan, 36.519 billion yuan and 122.626 billion yuan respectively, accounting for 4.10%, 22.00% and 73.89%. The average total liabilities of Zhongguancun NEEQ Listed Companies were 183 million yuan, an increase of 10.24% from 166 million yuan in 2019. Mainly due to the decrease in the number of Zhongguancun NEEQ Listed Companies in 2020 compared to 2019, although the total liabilities of Zhongguancun NEEQ Listed Companies decreased, their average total liabilities were on the rise.

(3) Asset-liability Ratio of Zhongguancun NEEQ Listed Companies in 2020

Solvency reflects the capability of an enterprise to pay its liabilities, which is an important capability to ensure the survival and development of the enterprise. From the point of view of the financial analysis, solvency includes short-term solvency and long-term solvency, and the report adopts the asset-liability ratio to evaluate the long-term solvency. According to the Standard Value of Enterprises Merit Evaluation-2020 published by the State-owned Assets Supervision and Administration Commission of the State Council (SASAC), the standard values for the asset-liability ratio under the industry-wide dimensions of state-owned enterprises nationwide are: 48.6% for excellent value, 53.6% for good value, 63.6% for average value, 73.6% for lower value, and 88.6% for poor value.

At the end of 2020, the overall asset-liability ratio of Zhongguancun NEEQ Listed Companies was 48.42%, down 1.90% from 2019, outperforming the overall asset-liability ratio of national NEEQ Listed Companies (60.34%). Among them, the asset-liability ratio of the Select, Innovation and Base were 46.47%, 43.12% and 50.38% respectively. The asset-liability ratios of the Select and Innovation were relatively excellent, while the asset-liability ratio of the Base was slightly higher.

According to the Standard Value of Enterprises Merit Evaluation-2020, among the entire Zhongguancun NEEQ Listed Companies, there were 565 enterprises with an asset-liability ratio below 48.6%, accounting for 61.95%; 60 enterprises with an asset-liability ratio between 48.6% and 53.6%, accounting for 6.58%; and 61 enterprises with an asset-liability ratio above 88.6%, accounting for 6.69% (see Table 4.2). The above data shows that more than 60% of Zhongguancun NEEQ Listed Companies have excellent value of asset-liability ratios, which means that the financial risk of these enterprises is low and their long-term solvency is guaranteed, but it also means that more than 60% of enterprises' bond financing is insufficient. In addition, less than 10% of Zhongguancun NEEQ Listed Companies have poor value of asset-liability ratios, which are particularly worthy of being regulated as their long-term solvency cannot be guaranteed and their risk is higher.

Table 4.2 Distribution of Zhongguancun NEEQ Listed Companies' Asset-liability ratio in 2020

Asset-liability ratio (%)	Number	Proportion (%)	Evaluation value
≤48.6	565	61.95	Excellent value
48.6–53.6	60	6.58	Good value
53.6–63.6	92	10.09	Average value
63.6–73.6	63	6.91	Lower value
73.6–88.6	71	7.79	Relatively poor value
>88.6	61	6.69	Poor value
Total	912	100.00	-

Source Wind, compiled by ZLCA

2. Analysis of Zhongguancun NEEQ Listed Companies' Cash Flow Liability Ratio[1] in 2020

In order to further explore the long-term solvency of Zhongguancun NEEQ Listed Companies, the report analyses the figure of cash flow liability ratio to reflect the capability of Zhongguancun NEEQ Listed Companies to use the net cash obtained from operating activities to repay all its liabilities. In terms of the meaning of the indicator, the higher the ratio, the stronger the capability to repay total liabilities.

In 2020, the cash flow liability ratio of Zhongguancun NEEQ Listed Companies was 4.15%, which was lower than the cash flow liability ratio of national NEEQ Listed Companies (8.69%), indicating that Zhongguancun NEEQ Listed Companies were not as capable of using net cash flow from operating activities to repay their total liabilities as national NEEQ Listed Companies. In addition, the cash flow liability ratio of Zhongguancun NEEQ Listed Companies in the Select was the highest at 18.22%, far exceeding the cash flow liability ratio of enterprises in the Innovation and the Base, which were 3.68% and 3.50% respectively.

In 2020, there were 351 enterprises (38.49%) with net cash flow from operating activities less than 0. These enterprises cannot use the net cash flow from operating activities to pay off their liabilities and were at risk; in addition, 373 enterprises (40.90%) had a cash flow liability ratio of 0 to 50% and can use the net cash flow from operating activities to pay off some liabilities; 93 enterprises (10.20%) had a cash flow liability ratio of 50% to 100%, and 95 enterprises (10.42%) had a cash flow liability ratio greater than or equal to 1, and these enterprises had a strong capability to repay their liabilities (see Table 4.3).

[1] cash flow liability ratio = (net cash obtained from operating activities/total liability) × 100%.

Table 4.3 Distribution of Zhongguancun NEEQ Listed Companies' cash flow liability ratio in 2020

Cash Flow Liability Ratio (%)	Number	Proportion (%)
<0	351	38.49
0–20	239	26.21
20%–50	134	14.69
50%–100	93	10.20
≥100	95	10.42
Total	912	100.00

Source Wind, compiled by ZLCA

3. Asset-Liability Ratio and Cash Flow Liability Ratio of Various Industries in 2020

As for various industries, there were 10 industries with a relatively good performance on asset-liability ratio (asset-liability ratio below 48.6%), namely Education, Mining, Residential services, Repairs and other services, Real estate, Manufacturing, Scientific research and technology service, Health and Social work, Financials, Information transmission, Software and IT services, and Culture, Sports and Entertainment. There were seven industries with cash flow liability ratio of more than 10%, namely Agriculture, Forestry, Animal husbandry and Fishery, Scientific research and technology service, Accommodation and Catering industry, Real estate, Scientific research and technology service, Manufacturing, Residential services, Repairs and other services (see Table 4.4).

4.1.3 Analysis of Zhongguancun NEEQ Listed Companies' Short-Term Solvency in 2020

1. Analysis of Zhongguancun NEEQ Listed Companies' Short-Term Solvency Stock Ratio in 2020

(1) Current Ratio

The current ratio is the ratio of current assets to current liabilities, indicating how many current assets are used as debt repayment guarantee for every 1 yuan of current liabilities. The current ratio is a relative number. If the value is too low, it indicates that the enterprise's short-term solvency is insufficient. If the value is too high, the enterprise may have capital idle problems. Generally speaking, the minimum reasonable current ratio for a manufacturing enterprise is considered to be 2.

In 2020, the overall current ratio of Zhongguancun NEEQ Listed Companies was 1.67, slightly higher than that of the national NEEQ Listed Companies (1.44). Among Zhongguancun NEEQ Listed Companies, the current ratio of enterprises

Table 4.4 Zhongguancun NEEQ Listed Companies' asset-liability ratio and cash flow liability ratio of various industries in 2020

Industry	Asset-liability ratio (%)	Cash flow liability ratio (%)
Education	29.23	−20.27
Mining	30.78	−12.59
Residential services, Repairs and other services	33.47	13.14
Real Estate	38.55	18.80
Manufacturing	38.82	14.04
Scientific research and technology service	39.34	16.54
Health and Social work	40.87	14.07
Financials	42.28	0.33
Information transmission, Software and IT services	47.59	2.67
Culture, Sports and Entertainment	48.06	−0.14
Transportation, Warehousing and Postal services	52.91	−94.80
Accommodation and Catering industry	54.30	15.40
Wholesale and Retail businesses	56.02	9.20
Management of Water Conservancy, Environment and Public Facilities	56.66	−0.75
Electricity, Heat, Gas and Water production and supply industry	58.85	8.71
Agriculture, Forestry, Animal husbandry and Fishery	59.12	43.50
Construction	63.44	8.05
Leasing and Business services	66.48	3.27
Overall	48.42	4.15

Source Wind, compiled by ZLCA

in the Select, Innovation and Base were 1.19, 1.88 and 1.62 respectively. The data shows that the current ratio of Zhongguancun NEEQ Listed Companies performed better than that of the nation, and their short-term solvency was secured. Meanwhile, the current ratio of the Select is relatively low.

After excluding the 2 Zhongguancun NEEQ Listed Companies whose current ratio data was missed, in 2020, there were 113 enterprises with a current ratio below 1, accounting for 12.42%; 320 enterprises with a current ratio between 1 and 2, accounting for 35.16%; 323 enterprises with a current ratio between 2 and 5, accounting for 35.49%; and 154 enterprises with a current ratio above 5, accounting

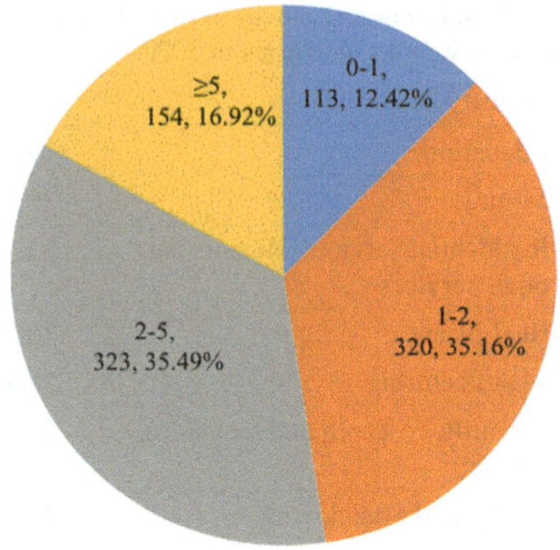

Fig. 4.2 Distribution of Zhongguancun NEEQ Listed Companies' current ratio in 2020. *Source* Wind, compiled by ZLCA

for 16.92%. The number of enterprises with a current ratio of 2 to 5 was 323, accounting for 35.49%; 154 enterprises with a current ratio of 5 or more, accounting for 16.92%. The above data shows that nearly 90% of Zhongguancun NEEQ Listed Companies have current ratios above 1, and their current assets are greater than their current liabilities, so they have the short-term solvency and are less likely to be insolvent in an embarrassing situation after an unexpected situation (see Fig. 4.2).

(2) Quick Ratio

The liquidity of the items constituting the current assets varies greatly, among which, inventories, prepayments and other non-quick assets are of great uncertainty in the realization amount and time of such assets. Therefore, quick assets are more credible as debt paying assets. For the above reasons, the report further reflects the short-term solvency of Zhongguancun NEEQ Listed Companies with quick ratio.

In 2020, the overall quick ratio of Zhongguancun NEEQ Listed Companies was 1.37, slightly higher than the national NEEQ Listed Companies' quick ratio (1.16). Among Zhongguancun NEEQ Listed Companies, the quick ratio of enterprises in the Select, Innovation and Base were 0.96, 1.46 and 1.37 respectively. The data shows that Zhongguancun NEEQ Listed Companies' quick ratios performed better than the national ones and had better short-term solvency. At the same time, the quick ratio of Zhongguancun NEEQ Listed Companies in the Select was lower than that of the Innovation and the Base.

After excluding the two Zhongguancun NEEQ Listed Companies with missing quick ratio data, in 2020, there were 213 enterprises with quick ratios below 1, accounting for 23.41%; 302 enterprises with quick ratios between 1 and 2, accounting for 33.19%; 223 enterprises with quick ratios between 2 and 4, accounting for 24.51%; 172 enterprises with quick ratios of 4 and above, accounting for 18.90%. The above figures show that nearly 80% of the enterprises had a quick ratio of 2 to 4, accounting for 24.51%. The above data shows that nearly 80% of Zhongguancun

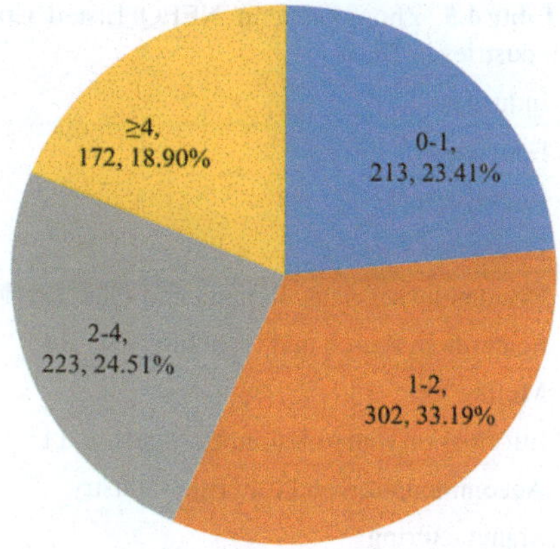

Fig. 4.3 Distribution of Zhongguancun NEEQ Listed Companies' quick ratio in 2020. *Source* Wind, compiled by ZLCA

NEEQ Listed Companies have a quick ratio above 1, indicating that the quick assets of these enterprises are greater than their current liabilities and have the capability to repay their current liabilities quickly (see Fig. 4.3).

(3) Cash Ratio

Among quick assets, the most liquid asset that can be directly used for debt repayment is cash. The report adopts cash ratio to further measure the short-term solvency of Zhongguancun NEEQ Listed Companies.

In 2020, there were 453 enterprises with a cash ratio below 0.5, accounting for 49.67%; 141 companies with a cash ratio between 0.5 and 1, accounting for 15.46%. 196 companies, accounting for 21.49%, had a cash ratio between 1 and 3. There were 122 companies with a cash ratio of more than 3, accounting for 13.38%. The above data shows that nearly 50% of Zhongguancun NEEQ Listed Companies have a cash ratio higher than 0.5, reflecting a good solvency (see Fig. 4.5).

2. Analysis of Zhongguancun NEEQ Listed Companies' Short-Term Solvency Stock Ratio of Various Industries in 2020

In general, 16 industries had a current ratio greater than 1, with five industries having a current ratio greater than 2, namely Education, Real Estate, Financials, Residential services, Repairs and other services and Mining. In addition, in terms of quick ratio, there were 14 industries with a current ratio greater than 1 and two industries with a quick ratio greater than 2, namely Education and Real Estate. On the whole, there were seven industries with current and quick ratios in the top 10, namely Education, Real Estate, Financials and Residential services, Repairs and other services, Scientific research and technology service, Mining, and Information transmission, Software and IT services (see Tables 4.4 and 4.5) (Fig. 4.4).

Table 4.5 Zhongguancun NEEQ Listed Companies' current ratio and quick ratio of various industries in 2020

Industry	Current ratio	Quick ratio
Education	2.6	2.46
Real Estate	2.02	2.01
Financials	2.05	1.88
Residential services, Repairs and other services	2.11	1.84
Scientific research and technology service	1.98	1.8
Mining	2.08	1.74
Information transmission, Software and IT services	1.87	1.59
Accommodation and Catering industry	1.39	1.39
Manufacturing	1.61	1.2
Management of Water Conservancy, Environment and Public Facilities	1.27	1.15
Leasing and Business services	1.17	1.15
Transportation, Warehousing and Postal services	1.24	1.09
Construction	1.19	1.07
Health and Social work	1.22	1.06
Culture, Sports and Entertainment	1.91	0.97
Wholesale and Retail businesses	1.73	0.92
Electricity, Heat, Gas and Water production and supply industry	0.85	0.68
Agriculture, Forestry, Animal husbandry and Fishery	0.44	0.32
Overall	**1.67**	**1.37**

Source Wind, compiled by ZLCA

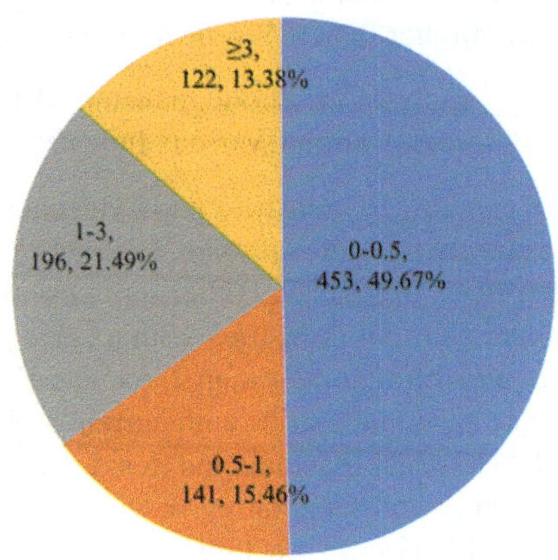

Fig. 4.4 Distribution of Zhongguancun NEEQ Listed Companies' cash ratio in 2020. *Source* Wind, compiled by ZLCA

4.2 Analysis of Zhongguancun NEEQ Listed Companies' Operating Capability in 2020

4.2.1 Operating Capability

Operating capability is a financial ratio to measure the efficiency of asset management, which affects the profitability and solvency of modern enterprises. Zhongguancun NEEQ Listed Companies are mainly science and technology innovative enterprises in the growth stage. Their rapid growth depends not only on breakthroughs in products and services brought about by technological research and development, but also on the efficiency of the enterprises' utilisation of assets. Therefore, an analysis of the operating capability of Zhongguancun NEEQ Listed Companies can help to assess the growth of enterprises from the perspective of their operational efficiency.

As operating capability is used to evaluate the efficiency of asset management, the indicators for measuring operating capability all reflect the investment of various assets required by an enterprise for every 1 yuan of revenue. For enterprises, the accounts receivable turnover ratio can reflect the collection speed of an enterprise's revenue; the inventory turnover ratio can evaluate the management of inventory and analyse the occupancy of capital by inventory; the fixed assets turnover ratio reflects how much fixed assets investment an enterprise needs for every 1 yuan of income, and whether the enterprise has the capability of light asset operation; the total assets turnover ratio is an overall assessment of an enterprise's operating capability. All of the above indicators are vital indicators for evaluating the operating capability of an enterprise, and the report uses the above indicators to systematically evaluate the operating capability of Zhongguancun NEEQ Listed Companies.

4.2.2 Analysis of Zhongguancun NEEQ Listed Companies' Accounts Receivable in 2020

1. Overall Status of Zhongguancun NEEQ Listed Companies' Accounts Receivable in 2020

As at December 31st, 2020, the total accounts receivable of Zhongguancun NEEQ Listed Companies was 46.452 billion yuan, a decrease of 16.64% compared with the previous year. The overall accounts receivable turnover days of Zhongguancun NEEQ Listed Companies in 2020 was 92.31 days, a decrease of 2.86 days compared with 2019. From the above data, it can be seen that both the number of total accounts receivable and the accounts receivable turnover days of Zhongguancun NEEQ Listed Companies have decreased, indicating that the enterprises' repayment situation has been gradually improved (see Fig. 4.5).

Excluding the 33 enterprises without accounts receivable turnover days, in 2020, among Zhongguancun NEEQ Listed Companies, the accounts receivable turnover

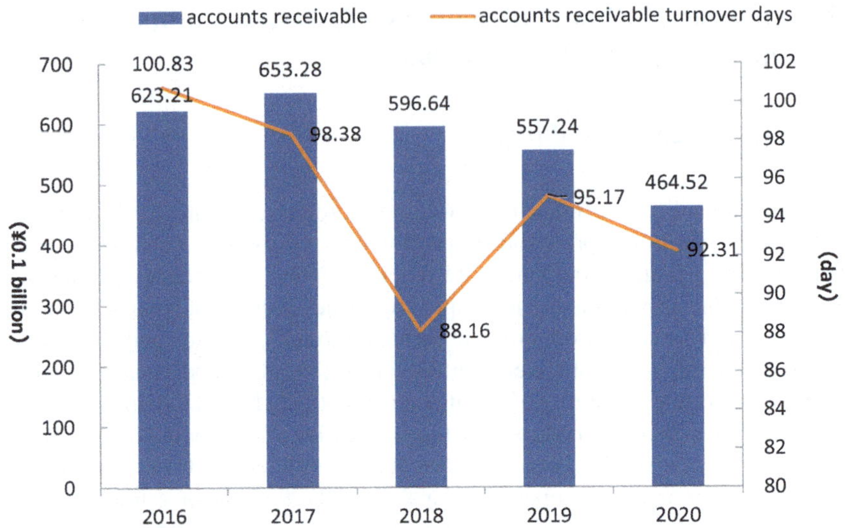

Fig. 4.5 Changes in Zhongguancun NEEQ Listed Companies' accounts receivable in 2020. *Source* Wind, compiled by ZLCA

days were 88.46 days of enterprises in the Select and 87.90 days of enterprises in the Innovation, which were basically the same as the accounts receivable turnover days of enterprises in the Select, while the accounts receivable turnover days of enterprises in the Base were higher than those of the Select and Innovation, at 104.06 days.

2. Distribution of Zhongguancun NEEQ Listed Companies' Accounts Receivable Turnover Days in 2020

Excluding the 33 enterprises without accounts receivable turnover days, there were 43 enterprises with accounts receivable turnover days less than 7 days, accounting for 4.89% of the total number of Zhongguancun NEEQ Listed Companies in 2020; 103 enterprises with accounts receivable turnover days between 7 and 30 days, accounting for 11.72% of the total number of Zhongguancun NEEQ Listed Companies; 237 enterprises with accounts receivable turnover days between 30 and 90 days, accounting for 26.96% of the total number of Zhongguancun NEEQ Listed Companies, whose frequency of accounts receivable turnover was between one month and one quarter; 226 enterprises with accounts receivable turnover days between 90 and 180 days, accounting for 25.71% of the total number of Zhongguancun NEEQ Listed Companies, whose frequency of accounts receivable turnover ranged from one quarter to half a year. There were 270 enterprises with accounts receivable turnover days of 180 days or above, accounting for 30.72% of the total number of Zhongguancun NEEQ Listed Companies. The turnover frequency of accounts receivable of these enterprises was relatively low, and the enterprises' capital was excessively suppressed in accounts receivable, which might affect the normal turnover of capital,

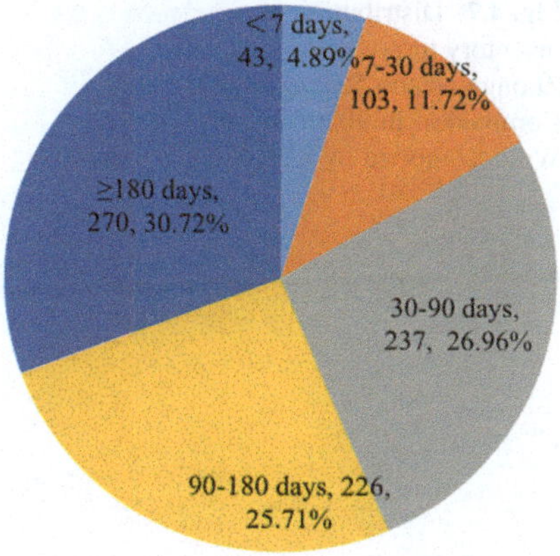

Fig. 4.6 Distribution of Zhongguancun NEEQ Listed Companies' accounts receivable turnover days in 2020. *Source* Wind, compiled by ZLCA

and might also affect the solvency and financial expenses of the enterprises (see Fig. 4.6).

4.2.3 Analysis of Zhongguancun NEEQ Listed Companies' Inventory Turnover Days in 2020

Excluding 171 enterprises without inventory turnover days data, the total inventory turnover days of Zhongguancun NEEQ Listed Companies in 2020 was 91.83 days, 29.91 days more than that of 2019 (61.92 days). Among them, the inventory turnover days of enterprises in the Select, Innovation and Base were 95.69 days, 74.64 days and 113.72 days respectively. This shows that the inventory turnover of Zhongguancun NEEQ Listed Companies in 2020 is lower than that in 2019, the conversion rate of inventory into cash through sales is slower, and the occupation level of inventory to capital is increased.

In 2020, there were 74 enterprises with inventory turnover days of less than 7 days, accounting for 9.99% of the total number of Zhongguancun NEEQ Listed Companies; 82 enterprises with inventory turnover days of 7 to 30 (excluding 30) days, accounting for 11.07% of the total number of Zhongguancun NEEQ Listed Companies; 163 enterprises with inventory turnover days of 30 to 90 (excluding 90) days, accounting for 22.00% of the total number of Zhongguancun NEEQ Listed Companies; the number of enterprises with inventory turnover days between 90 and 180 (excluding 180) days was 175, accounting for 23.62% of the total number of Zhongguancun NEEQ Listed Companies; and the number of enterprises with inventory turnover days of 180 days and above was 247, accounting for 33.33% of the total number of Zhongguancun NEEQ Listed Companies (see Fig. 4.7).

In summary, in 2020, about 20% of the enterprises' inventory turnover days was less than one month, reflecting a high inventory turnover efficiency and a strong

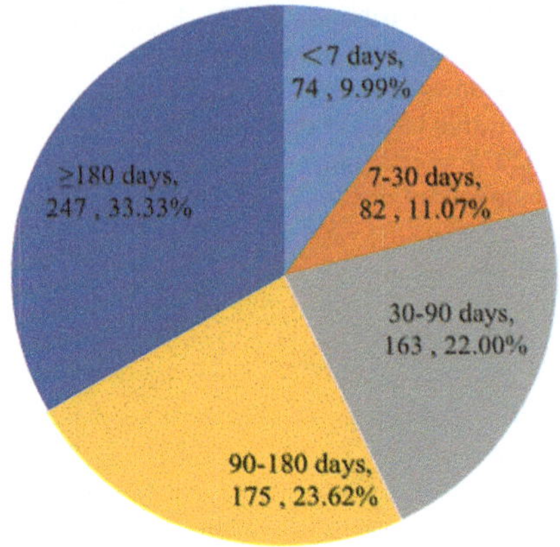

Fig. 4.7 Distribution of inventory turnover days of Zhongguancun NEEQ Listed Companies' in 2020. *Source* Wind, compiled by ZLCA

inventory management capability, while there were also about 30% of enterprises with a low inventory turnover efficiency.

4.2.4 Analysis of Zhongguancun NEEQ Listed Companies' Fixed Assets Turnover Days in 2020

Excluding the 20 companies without fixed assets turnover days, the overall fixed assets turnover days of Zhongguancun NEEQ Listed Companies in 2020 was 35.85 days, an increase of 0.8 days from 2019 (35.05 days); the overall fixed assets turnover days for enterprises in the Select, Innovation and Base were 132.77 days, 19.50 days and 43.08 days respectively.

In 2020, there were 372 enterprises with fixed assets turnover days of less than 7 days, accounting for 41.70% of the total number of Zhongguancun NEEQ Listed Companies; 212 enterprises with fixed assets turnover days of 7 days to 30 days, accounting for 23.77% of the total number of Zhongguancun NEEQ Listed Companies; 138 enterprises with fixed assets turnover days of 30 days to 90 days, accounting for 15.47%; 72 enterprises with fixed assets turnover days between 90 and 180 days, accounting for 8.07% of the total number of Zhongguancun NEEQ Listed Companies; and 98 enterprises with fixed assets turnover days of 180 days or more, accounting for 10.99% of the total number of Zhongguancun NEEQ Listed Companies (see Fig. 4.8).

Overall, the number of fixed assets turnover days of Zhongguancun NEEQ Listed Companies increased slightly in 2020, which indicated a decrease in the efficiency of fixed assets utilisation of the Zhongguancun NEEQ Listed Companies. In addition, the fixed assets turnover days of enterprises in the Select were also much higher than those of the Innovation and the Base.

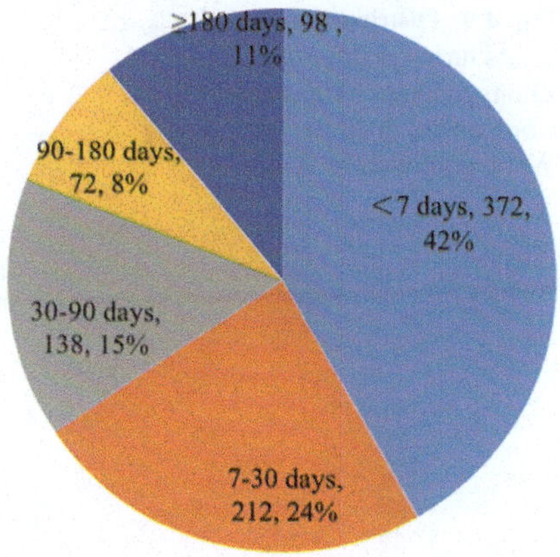

Fig. 4.8 Distribution of fixed assets turnover days of Zhongguancun NEEQ Listed Companies' in 2020. *Source* Wind, compiled by ZLCA

4.2.5 Analysis of Zhongguancun NEEQ Listed Companies' Total Assets Turnover Days in 2020

Excluding the 15 enterprises without total assets turnover days, the overall total assets turnover days of Zhongguancun NEEQ Listed Companies in 2020 was 664.04 days, a decrease of 2.91 days from 2019 (666.95 days); the total assets turnover days of enterprises in the Select, Innovation and Base were 631.21 days, 330.86 days and 994.60 days respectively.

In 2020, there were 68 enterprises with total assets turnover days of less than 180 days, accounting for 7.58% of the total number of Zhongguancun NEEQ Listed Companies; 221 enterprises with total assets turnover days of 180 to 360 (excluding 360) days, accounting for 24.64% of the total number of Zhongguancun NEEQ Listed Companies; 173 enterprises with total assets turnover days of 360 to 540 (excluding 540) days, accounting for 19.29% of the total number of Zhongguancun NEEQ Listed Companies; 130 enterprises with total assets turnover days of 540 to 720 (excluding 720) days, accounting for 14.49% of the total number of Zhongguancun NEEQ Listed Companies; and the number of enterprises with total assets turnover days of 720 days and above was 305, accounting for 34.00% of the total number of Zhongguancun NEEQ Listed Companies.

The above data shows that nearly 70% of Zhongguancun NEEQ Listed Companies can recoup their total assets investment through revenue within two years. It can be seen that, in addition to some enterprises showing a high level of asset operating capability, the overall asset operating capability of Zhongguancun NEEQ Listed Companies is also at the middle to upper level (see Fig. 4.9).

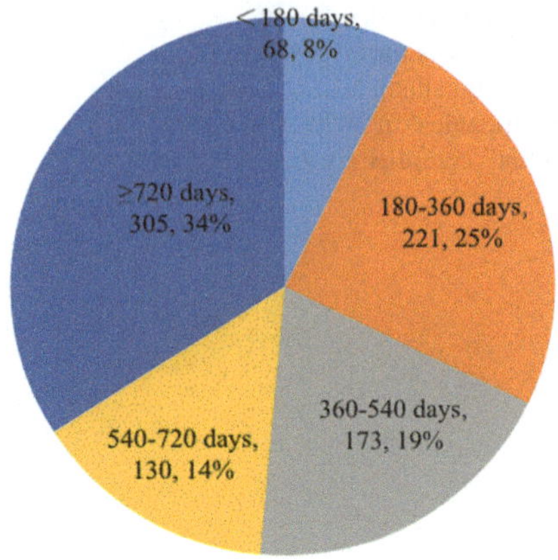

Fig. 4.9 Distribution of total assets turnover days of Zhongguancun NEEQ Listed Companies' in 2020. *Source* Wind, compiled by ZLCA

4.3 Conclusions and Recommendations

The above analysis of Zhongguancun NEEQ Listed Companies' solvency shows that the overall debt ratio of Zhongguancun NEEQ Listed Companies is moderate, with 60% of them having a strong long-term solvency, but their asset-liability ratios are low, reflecting the ineffective use of financial leverage; the cash flow debt ratio is lower than that of national NEEQ Listed Companies, and there is a polarization phenomenon. Some enterprises are not good at using the cash inflows from operating activities to repay the debt, and there are also some enterprises whose net cash flows from operating activities are much higher than the total liabilities, reflecting the fact that these enterprises have not planned their liabilities properly, resulting in excessive financial risks or idle cash assets. The current ratio and quick ratio of different industries are generally better than the average of the corresponding industries on the national NEEQ Listed Companies, demonstrating a strong short-term solvency.

At the same time, the analysis of the operating capability of Zhongguancun NEEQ Listed Companies shows that the total number of both accounts receivable and the accounts receivable turnover days decreases, and the management efficiency of accounts receivable increases. But there are still some enterprises with long collection cycle of accounts receivable, which may affect the solvency of enterprises. The fixed assets turnover days are relatively low, which highlights the improvement of the overall management efficiency of Zhongguancun NEEQ Listed Companies. Most Zhongguancun NEEQ Listed Companies performed well in terms of total assets turnover days, and nearly 70% enterprises are able to recover their total asset investment through revenue within two years, resulting in a strong overall operating capability.

In response to the above findings and in light of characteristics of the economic development environment in 2020, the following recommendations are advisable.

(1) Enterprises should strengthen capital management to ensure the rational and effective use of company funds. At the same time, a long-term effective

accounts receivable management mechanism should be established to help enterprises improve the efficiency of capital. On the premise of protecting the shareholders' interests, financing channels should be enriched and rationally use financial leverage to meet the necessary capital needs of enterprises.

(2) The management of operating capital, to which the managerial personnel of an enterprise should attach importance through the financial administration, is related to the solvency and operating capability of an enterprise. Measures such as formulating appropriate credit policies, optimizing the amount of inventory purchase and storage, and making reasonable use of commercial credit financing should be taken to control the amount of operating capital, the efficiency of accounts receivable turnover and the efficiency of inventory turnover at an optimal level, in order to ensure the sufficient liquidity and safety of enterprises' financial status, achieve the efficiency of operating capital, and then promote the business performance.

Chapter 5
Comparative Analysis of the Overall Development of the NEEQ in Key Regions in 2020

5.1 Comparative Analysis of the Overall Situation of Each Region

As of the end of 2020, the total number of National NEEQ Listed Companies was 8,187, a decrease of 8.56% from 8,953 at the end of 2019. The top five regions for the number are Guangdong (1181), Zhongguancun (1073), Jiangsu (986), Zhejiang (713), and Shanghai (646), which has shown a certain degree of decline. In 2020, the total number in these five regions is 4,599, accounting for 56.18% of that number in the whole country (Table 5.1). This set of data shows that Guangdong, Zhongguancun, Jiangsu, Zhejiang, and Shanghai have ranked among the top five in the country for the number of NEEQ companies for consecutive years with obvious advantages.

As of April 30st, 2021, the number of NEEQ companies in Guangdong, Zhongguancun, Jiangsu, Zhejiang, and Shanghai that have published annual reports are 981, 912, 853, 619, and 533, respectively. The following takes the data disclosed in the annual report as the research object.

5.1.1 *Market Value*

In 2020, the total market value of Zhongguancun NEEQ enterprises was 292.676 billion yuan, and the total regional market values of Guangdong, Jiangsu, Zhejiang, and Shanghai were 304.33 billion yuan, 2.127536 billion yuan,[1] (217.764 billion

---

[1] The total market value of the newly listed company in Jiangsu Province in 2020, CHANGZHOU ZHUYOU DISPLAY S&T CO., LTD, is estimated to be 1909.772 billion yuan at the end of 2020,

Zhongguancun Listed Companies Association, *The Growth Report of Zhongguancun NEEQ Listed Companies (2021)*, Current Chinese Economic Report Series,
https://doi.org/10.1007/978-981-19-1242-9_5

Table 5.1 Number of NEEQ Companies in major regions in the country (Unit: Number, %)

Region	End of 2020		End of 2019		Growth rate	Number of enterprises with continued operations in 2019–2020
	Amount	Ratio	Amount	Ratio	Amount	
Guangdong	1181	14.43	1319	14.73	−10.46	972
Zhongguancun	1073	13.11	1190	13.29	−9.83	898
Jiangcun	986	12.04	1072	11.97	−8.02	825
Zhejiang	713	8.71	786	8.78	−9.29	606
Shanghai	646	7.89	715	7.99	−9.65	529

Source Wind, compiled by ZLCA

Table 5.2 The market value of NEEQ companies in major regions across the country (Unit: 100 million yuan, %)

	Companies disclosed anual report			Companies with continued operation		
	2020	2019	Growth rate	2020	2019	Growth rate
Zhongguancun	2926.73	3126.14	−6.38	2918.28	2745.81	6.28
Guangdong	3043.30	2768.89	9.91	3041.56	2467.53	23.26
Jiangsu	2177.64	1836.47	18.58	2123.28	1726.58	22.98
Zhejiang	2043.19	1635.1	24.96	2034.98	1493.91	36.22
Shanghai	1900.18	1975.9	−3.83	1896.88	1497.71	26.65

Source Wind, compiled by ZLCA

yuan after excluding extreme value), 204.319 billion yuan, and 190.18 billion yuan (Table 5.2). Relatively speaking, the market value of Zhongguancun and Guangdong have been in the forefront for two consecutive years. The total market value of companies with continuing operations in these five regions has increased to varying degrees. Among them, that of Zhejiang and Shanghai NEEQ companies has grown fast, indicating that the quality of companies with continuing operations is steadily improving (Fig. 5.1). In terms of the number of companies with a market value of no less than 5 billion yuan, Zhongguancun and Guangdong each have 7 companies, ranking first and Zhejiang 4, Shanghai 3 and Jiangsu 2 (Table 5.3).

accounting for 89.76% of the total market value of the enterprises disclosed in the annual report of Jiangsu Province. The company's main business focuses on the field of display equipment products. Focusing on the market dynamics, the company keeps tracking and analyzing customers' consumption trends, increasing research and development strength. It is mainly engaged in display equipment research and development: display props, furniture, packaging materials design, manufacturing and sales etc. The company adopts a procurement model of production-to-order. Excluding Zhuyou, the total market value of Jiangsu NEEQ listed companies is 217.764 billion yuan.

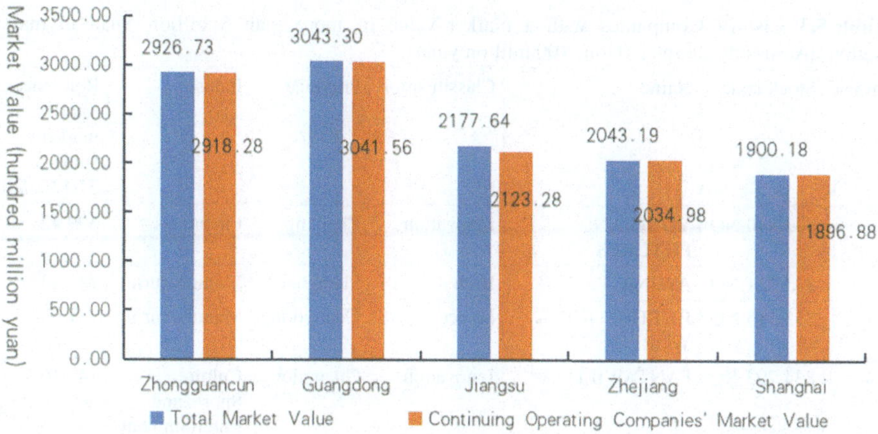

Fig. 5.1 The market value of the NEEQ enterprises in each region at the end of 2020. *Source* Wind, compiled by ZLCA

5.1.2 Asset

Zhongguancun NEEQ companies ranked first in the total assets and average total assets. In 2020, the total assets of Zhongguancun NEEQ companies were 342.753 billion yuan, ranking first; The second is the NEEQ enterprises in Jiangsu, with total assets of 311.774 billion yuan; followed by Guangdong, Zhejiang, and Shanghai, respectively, with total assets of 265.852 billion yuan, 203.908 billion yuan and 180.134 billion. From the perspective of average total assets, that of Zhongguancun enterprises in 2020 is 376 million yuan, ranking first. From the perspective of growth rate, the growth of Zhongguancun enterprises' assets is not dominant (Table 5.4).

Judging from the NEEQ companies that have been operating continuously for two consecutive years from 2019 to 2020, the total assets of continuing operations in Guangdong, Jiangsu, Zhejiang, and Shanghai have all increased by more than 10%. The total assets of continuing operations in Zhongguancun have increased slightly, which is only 1.30%. However, the total assets of Zhongguancun continuing operations in 2019 and 2020 are both ranked first.

5.1.3 Financing

5.1.3.1 Stock Issuance

According to the data disclosed by NEEQ, the total amount of financing from the stock issuance of National NEEQ Listed Companies was 33.85 billion yuan in 2020, an increase of 27.91% from 2019 (26.463 billion yuan). Similarly, the scale of financing in the five major regions has also improved. Among them, Zhongguancun,

Table 5.3 List of Companies with a market value of more than 5 billion Yuan in major regionsaAcross the country (Unit: 100 million yuan)

Rank	Stock code	Name	Classification	Province	Industry	Reference total market value 31/12/2020
1	833,840.NQ	YONG AN FUTURES	Innovation	Zhejiang	Financials	399.42
2	833,221.NQ	AWINIC	Base	Shanghai	Manufacturing	243.43
3	835,185.NQ	BETTER OUR WORLD	Select	Guangdong	Manufacturing	187.65
4	834,793.NQ	FANTAWILD	Innovation	Guangdong	Culture, Sports and Entertainment	147.16
5	831,200.NQ	JU ZHENG YUAN	Innovation	Guangdong	Wholesale and Retail businesses	124.42
6	832,970.NQ	DONGHAI SECURITIES	Base	Jiangsu	Financials	108.55
7	835,092.NQ	BANKSTEEL.COM	Innovation	Shanghai	Information transmission, Software and IT services	98.75
8	870,488.NQ	GUODU SECURITIES	Base	Beijing	Financials	96.78
9	832,898.NQ	TIANDI NO.1	Innovation	Guangdong	Manufacturing	87.73
10	834,089.NQ	ZSVC	Base	Zhejiang	Financials	86.56
11	832,397.NQ	HENGSHEN CO.,LTD	Innovation	Jiangsu	Manufacturing	82.45
12	832,793.NQ	COWIN CAPITAL	Base	Guangdong	Financials	75.54
13	870,972.NQ	CANTON TOWER	Base	Guangdong	Management of Water Conservancy, Environment and Public Facilities	74.41
14	430,719.NQ	TCJDCAPITAL	Base	Beijing	Financials	70.50
15	833,858.NQ	CHINAEQUITY	Base	Beijing	Financials	68.63
16	833,819.NQ	NUTRICHEM	Select	Beijing	Manufacturing	67.17
17	430,005.NQ	HTA	Innovation	Beijing	Manufacturing	59.86
18	834,678.NQ	EASTDAY.COM	Innovation	Shanghai	Information transmission, Software and IT services	59.82

(continued)

Table 5.3 (continued)

Rank	Stock code	Name	Classification	Province	Industry	Reference total market value 31/12/2020
19	830,899.NQ	YUEKAI SECURITIES	Innovation	Guangdong	Financials	59.71
20	430,277.NQ	SHENGSHANG EDUCATION	Innovation	Beijing	Leasing and Business services	58.35
21	837,512.NQ	HJDQ	Base	Zhejiang	Manufacturing	58.05
22	832,924.NQ	BRIGHTSTONE	Innovation	Beijing	Manufacturing	54.93
23	834,189.NQ	HUITONG	Base	Zhejiang	Manufacturing	52.36

Source Wind, compiled by ZLCA

Table 5.4 The total assets of the NEEQ Enterprises in each region in 2020 (Unit: 100 million yuan, %)

Region	Companies disclosed anual report				Companies with continued operation		
	2020	2019	Growth rate	2020 average total assets	2020	2019	Growth rate
Zhongguancun	3,427.53	3,376.80	1.50	3.76	3,403.92	3,360.19	1.30
Guangdong	2,658.52	2,416.28	10.03	2.71	2,648.54	2,407.84	10.00
Jiangsu	3,117.74	2,816.90	10.68	3.66	3,060.01	2,767.80	10.56
Zhejiang	2,039.08	1,778.17	14.67	3.29	2,027.68	1,769.00	14.62
Shanghai	1,801.34	1,522.19	18.34	3.38	1,792.03	1,514.19	18.35

Source Wind, compiled by ZLCA

Zhejiang, and Shanghai have seen substantial increases in both the number of stock issuances and the scale of financing. Zhongguancun's stock has been issued 82 times, with a financing amount of 5.979 billion yuan (a year-on-year increase of 45.86%); that of Jiangsu is 97 times, which is the most of five regions, with a financing amount of 3.963 billion yuan (26.17% lower than the same period last year); Guangdong, Zhejiang, and Shanghai's stock issuance financing amounts in 2020 were 4.507 billion yuan, 2.277 billion yuan, and 2.172 billion yuan (table 5.5).

From the perspective of stock issuance methods, Zhongguancun NEEQ companies have conducted a total of 70 private issuances in 2020, with an additional issuance of 758 million shares and a financing amount of 3.805 billion yuan. Zhongguancun NEEQ companies have implemented Equity Private Placement in a certain degree of growth in 2020 compared with 2019. Like Zhongguancun, Zhejiang and Shanghai have seen a certain increase in the times and number of issuances and the amount

Table 5.5 The stock issuance in major regions in 2020 (Unit: times,100 million yuan, %)

Province	2020		2019		Growth rate	
	Times	Amount	Times	Amount	Times	Amount
Zhongguancun	82	59.79	79	40.99	3.80	45.86
Guangdong	83	45.07	91	36.87	-8.79	22.24
Jiangsu	97	39.63	92	53.68	5.43	-26.17
Zhejiang	66	22.77	47	13.22	40.43	72.24
Shanghai	54	21.72	53	13.66	1.89	59.00

Source NEEQ, compiled by ZLCA

Table 5.6 Comparison of equity private placement of NEEQ companies in major regions in 2020

Region	Number of equity private placement		Amount of equity private placement		Financing amount	
	Times (time)	Growth rate (%)	Amount (100 million shares)	Growth rate (%)	Amount (100 million yuan)	Growth rate (%)
Zhongguancun	70	4.48	7.58	8.34	38.05	1.75
Guangdong	74	-12.94	5.73	44.73	28.88	51.45
Jiangsu	84	1.20	4.29	-84.97	20.99	-64.42
Zhejiang	48	14.29	3.63	15.14	15.55	11.51
Shanghai	58	26.09	3.37	45.84	15.59	18.79

Source Wind, compiled by ZLCA

of financing. The two places have issued additional 48 and 58 times respectively, raising funds of 1.555 billion yuan and 1.559 billion yuan. Although the number of Equity Private Placement in Guangdong has decreased, the amount of funds raised has risen sharply. In 2020, 2.888 billion yuan was raised, a year-on-year increase of 51.45%; Jiangsu NEEQ companies raised relatively less funds through Equity Private Placement in 2020 (Table 5.6).

5.1.3.2 Bond Issuance

In 2020, a total of 7 NEEQ companies issued 11 bonds, with a total financing of 9.12 billion yuan. Among them, three companies in Zhongguancun, which are I&G, CAPITAL AIR, and CKFIL, issued bonds for 3 times with a total scale 3.65 billion yuan and an average coupon rate of 4.99%; 3 companies in Zhejiang issued bonds 5 times with a scale of 30.2 100 million yuan and an average coupon rate of 5.49%. Guangdong, Jiangsu, and Shanghai NEEQ companies have no bond issuance in 2020 (Table 5.7). In 2020, the number of Zhongguancun NEEQ companies for bond financing and the actual amount of financing accounted for 27.27% and 40.02% of

Table 5.7 National bond issuance in 2020

	Securities code	Enterpries code	Province	Coupon rate (%)	Scale (100 million yuan)	Term (year)	Enterprise attributes	Use of raised funds
1	177,451.SH	806,667.NQ	Zhejiang	5.90	5.00	3	State-owned enterprise	Repay loans from financial institutions
2	175,368.SH	880,090.NQ	Heilongjiang	6.50	10.00	5	State-owned enterprise	Repay the company's due debts
3	167,733.SH	806,667.NQ	Zhejiang	5.60	7.00	3	State-owned enterprise	Repay loans from financial institutions
4	175,051.SH	834,777.NQ	Beijing	4.47	30.00	3	State-owned enterprise	Repay interest-bearing debts, optimize debt structure, supplement working capital, etc
5	175.47.SH	880,090.NQ	Heilongjiang	6.50	10.00	5	State-owned enterprise	Repay the company's due debts
6	166,767.SH	805,865.NQ	Zhejiang	5.35	10.00	7	State-owned enterprise	All will be used for the construction project of Hengjin Industrial Park
7	166,640.SH	891,213.NQ	Zhejiang	4.20	0.60	3	State-owned enterprise	It will be used in the ETC construction and renovation project and supplementary working capital of Zhejiang Taizhou Expressway Group Co., Ltd
8	166,668.SH	832,496.NQ	Beijing	4.00	1.50	3	State-owned enterprise	Repay interest-bearing debts and supplement working capital

(continued)

Table 5.7 (continued)

	Securities code	Enterpries code	Province	Coupon rate (%)	Scale (100 million yuan)	Term (year)	Enterprise attributes	Use of raised funds
9	166,494.SH	806,667.NQ	Zhejiang	6.40	7.60	5	State-owned enterprise	Repay loans from financial institutions
10	166,158.SH	880,090.NQ	Heilongjiang	7.30	4.50	5	State-owned enterprise	Supplement the company's liquidity and repay the company's due debts
11	166,190.SH	833,499.NQ	Beijing	6.50	5.00	3	public enterprise	It is planned to use 120 million yuan to invest in direct lease projects for enterprises which provide support for epidemic prevention work; 880 million yuan will be used to repay debts

Source Wind, compiled by ZLCA

Table 5.8 NEEQ Enterprise income tax in major region in 2020 (Unit: 100 million yuan, %)

Region	Enterprises income tax in annual disclosed report			Companies with continue operations		
	2020	2019	Growth rate	Income tax in 2020	Average enterprise income tax in 2020	Growth rate of average enterprise income tax in 2020
Zhongguancun	20.02	18.35	9.14	19.91	221.75	8.88
Guangdong	18.98	17.76	6.89	18.92	194.60	7.04
Jiangsu	24.75	17.56	40.89	23.98	290.67	40.05
Zhejiang	20.99	16.76	25.28	20.86	344.30	25.20
Shanghai	10.87	7.01	55.02	10.66	201.46	55.10

Source Wind, compiled by ZLCA

the country's total, which is much higher than other regions. In the absence of not active bond financing in the overall NEEQ market, the performance of Zhongguancun NEEQ companies is better than other regions.

5.1.4 *Tax*

5.1.4.1 Enterprise Income Tax

In 2020, Zhongguancun NEEQ Companies income tax payment totals 2.02 billion yuan, which is lower only than Jiangsu and Zhejiang. The total tax payment of Zhongguancun companies with continuing operations in 2020 is 1.99 billion yuan, an increase of 8.88% year-on-year. From the perspective of the average income tax paid by companies with continuing operations, in 2020 that in Zhongguancun, Guangdong, Jiangsu, Zhejiang, and Shanghai increase to varying degrees. Jiangsu and Shanghai have the highest increase in income tax, respectively 40.05% and 55.10%. Relatively speaking, Zhongguancun's income tax increase is relatively small, with an average income tax of 2.2175 million yuan, a year-on-year increase of 8.88% (Table 5.8).

5.1.4.2 Actual Tax Burden

The actual tax burden of Zhongguancun NEEQ companies in 2020 is 5.769 billion yuan, which is 19.16% lower than the 7.137 billion yuan in 2019 and it is the largest drop. The actual tax burdens of Guangdong, Jiangsu, Zhejiang, and Shanghai are 4.833 billion yuan, 6.45 billion yuan, 3.661 billion yuan, and 3.815 billion yuan,

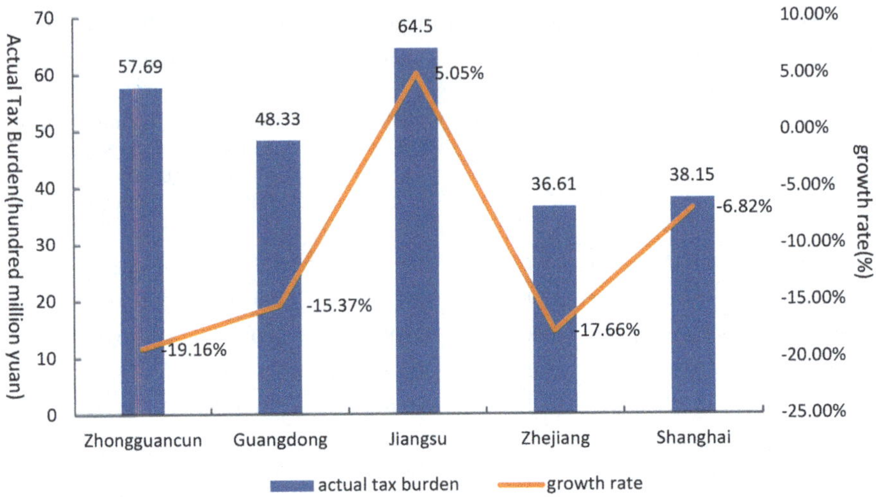

Fig. 5.2 The actual tax burden of NEEQ Companies in each major region in 2020. *Source* Wind, compiled by ZLCA

respectively, all of which decreased to a certain extent. Overall, the actual tax burden of major regional enterprises continued to decline (Fig. 5.2). From the perspective of the average actual tax burden of enterprises, the average actual tax burden of Zhongguancun and Zhejiang have droped significantly in 2020. Among them, the average actual tax burden of Zhongguancun has droped from 6,602,200 yuan to 6,326,200 yuan (Fig. 5.3). That in Guangdong was basically the same, with a slight increase, but that in Jiangsu and Shanghai rose sharply. Overall, the average actual tax burden of NEEQ enterprises in Shanghai and Jiangsu is relatively heavy.

From the perspective of the actual tax burden as a percentage of revenue, it continued to decline in the other four regions, except Shanghai. Among them, the actual tax burden of Zhongguancun NEEQ companies as a proportion of revenue fell from 3.77% in 2019 to 3.13% in 2020, a decrease of 0.64 percentage points (Table 5.9). However, compared to several other regions, that is just second to Jiangsu, whose percent is 3.84%, but it is much higher than that of the other three regions. In summary, the actual tax burden of Zhongguancun's NEEQ enterprises still has room for further reduction.

5.1.5 Staff Composition

5.1.5.1 Number of Employees

In 2020, the number of employees of Zhongguancun NEEQ companies was 144,900, which was only higher than that in Shanghai NEEQ companies (106,800). The total number of employees of Guangdong, Jiangsu and Zhejiang NEEQ companies in 2020 are 241,200, 194,500, and 152,300. From the perspective of growth rate, the number

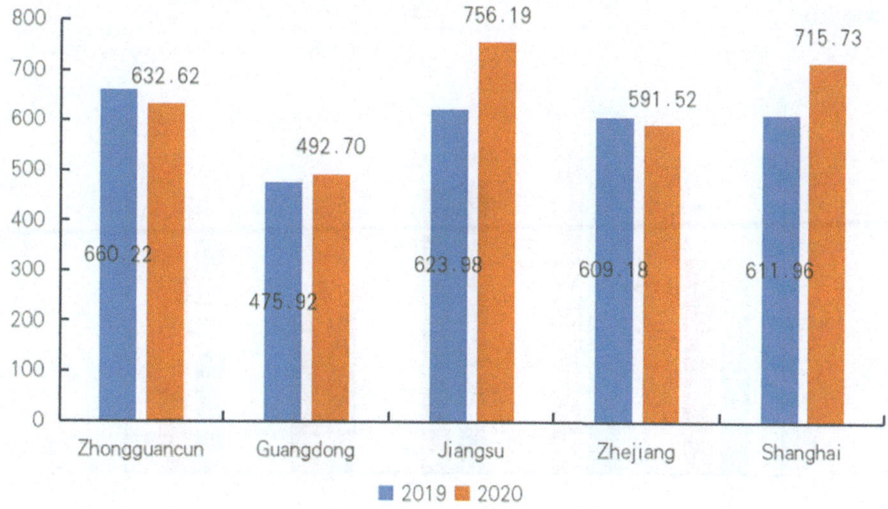

Fig. 5.3 Comparison of average actual tax burdens of NEEQ Companies in major regions from 2019 to 2020. *Source* Wind, compiled by ZLCA

Table 5.9 The revenue and the proportion of actual tax burden to revenue of NEEQ companies in major regions in 2020

Region	Revenue		Proportion of actual tax burden to revenue (%)	
	Amount (100 million yuan)	Growth rate (%)	2020	2019
Zhongguancun	1840.75	−2.73	3.13	3.77
Guangdong	1728.13	6.70	2.80	3.53
Jiangsu	1681.71	8.13	3.84	3.95
Zhejiang	1665.62	8.21	2.20	2.89
Shanghai	1834.38	−25.03	2.08	1.67

Source Wind, compiled by ZLCA

of employees in Zhongguancun NEEQ companies dropped by 15.28%. Guangdong, Zhejiang, and Shanghai continued the trend of employee reduction in 2019, with a decline of more than 10%. The total number of employees in Jiangsu NEEQ companies in 2020 still shows a downward trend, but the decline has slowed down (Fig. 5.4).

Judging from the number of employees of the NEEQ companies that have been operating for two consecutive years from 2019 to 2020, the total number of employees in the NEEQ companies in Zhongguancun, Guangdong, Jiangsu, Zhejiang, and Shanghai have also declined to a certain extent. Relatively speaking, that decline

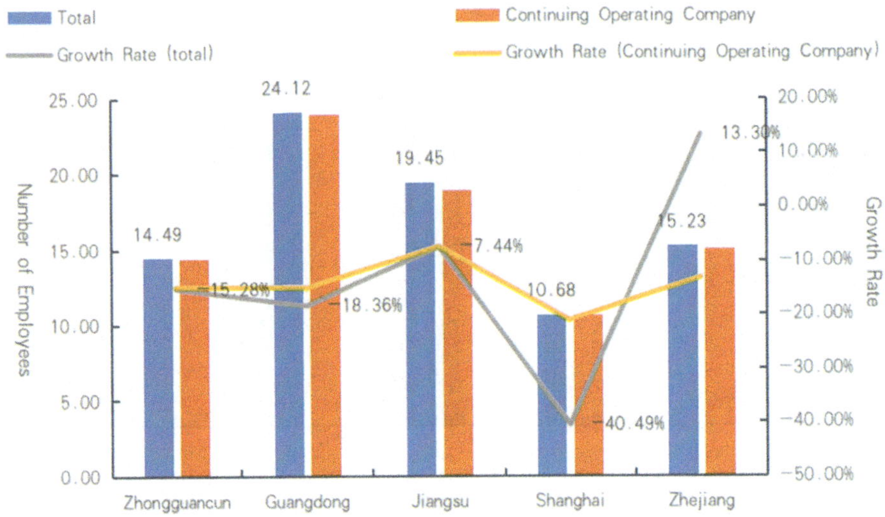

Fig. 5.4 Total number of employees of NEEQ Companies in each major region in 2020. *Source* Wind, compiled by ZLCA

in Jiangsu is the smallest in the five regions. The number of employees in Zhejiang companies with continuing operations is on the rise.

5.1.5.2 Staff Education Background

In 2020, Zhongguancun NEEQ companies have 68,400 undergraduates, masters and doctors (59,400 undergraduates, 8456 masters, and 540 doctors), accounting for 47.20% of the employees. The average number of undergraduates, masters, and doctors is 75; Guangdong occupies the second place with a total number of 56 million (50,994 undergraduates, 4585 masters, and 360 doctors), accounting for 23.36% and the average number is 57. The total number of undergraduates, masters, and Ph.Ds in Jiangsu, Zhejiang and Shanghai is respectively 40,500, 28,400, and 40,800 (Fig. 5.5). The data shows that the overall academic qualifications of employees in Zhongguancun NEEQ are better than those in other regions. Both the each number of undergraduates, masters, doctors, and the total number are significantly higher than other regions. Zhongguancun NEEQ companies can attract talents with higher education, which makes the employees have higher quality and stronger competitiveness.

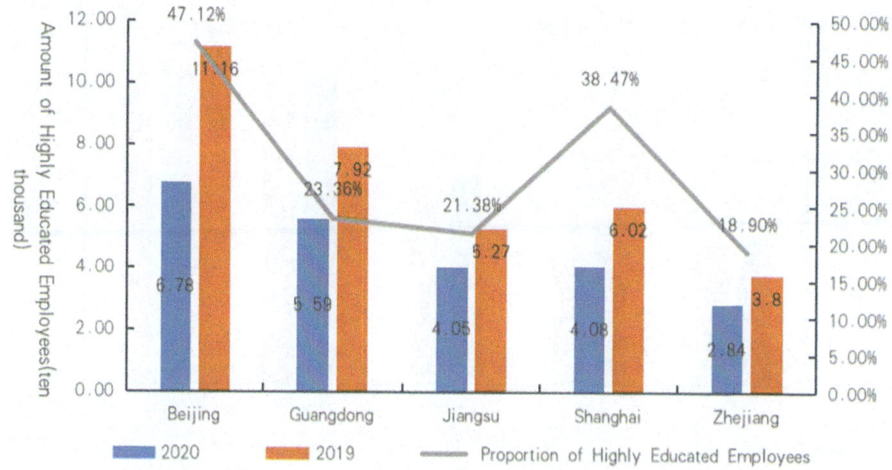

Fig. 5.5 The number and proportion of undergraduates, masters and Ph.Ds in NEEQ Companies in major regions in 2020. *Source* Wind, compiled by ZLCA

5.2 Analysis of Profitability of NEEQ Enterprises in Various Regions

5.2.1 Revenue

In 2020, the total revenue of Zhongguancun NEEQ companies is 184.075 billion yuan, which is higher than that of other major regions. The total revenue of Shanghai, Guangdong, Jiangsu, and Zhejiang was 183.438 billion yuan, 172.813 billion yuan, 168.171 billion yuan, and 166.562 billion yuan respectively. In addition, the total revenue of the five regions has declined to varying degrees. Among them, Shanghai and Zhejiang have the highest degree of decline, which are 30.84% and 24.06%, respectively. That of Zhongguancun NEEQ companies has fallen by 10.94%. From the perspective of average revenue, the average revenue of Shanghai NEEQ companies in 2020 is ahead of other regions, reaching 344 million yuan. Guangdong has the lowest average revenue of 176 million yuan; Zhongguancun NEEQ companies' average revenue is in the middle position, which is 202 million yuan.

Judging from the total revenue of the NEEQ companies that have been operating continuously for two consecutive years from 2019 to 2020, three of the five regions have increased their total revenue, Zhongguancun has a slight decline (-2.99%), and Shanghai has a large decline, a year-on-year decrease of 25.21% (Fig. 5.6).

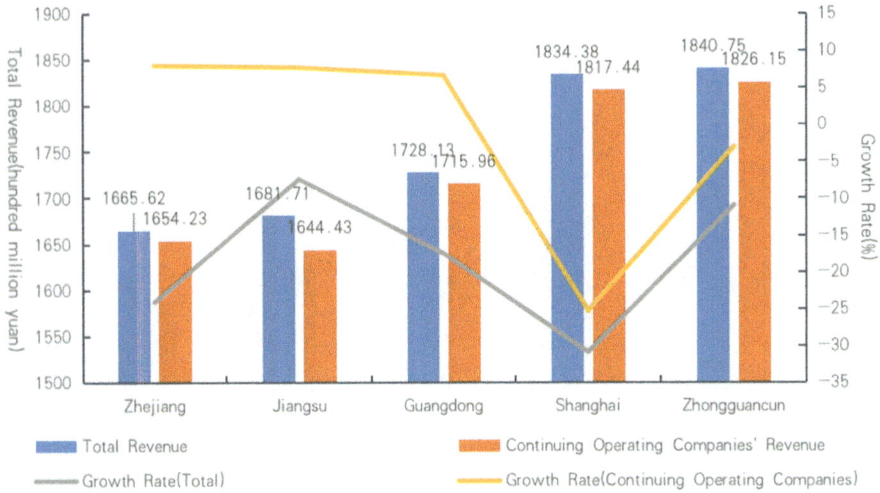

Fig. 5.6 The total and continuing revenue of NEEQ Companies in each major region in 2020. *Source* Wind, compiled by ZLCA

5.2.2 *Net Profit*

In 2020, affected by a few companies[2] with huge losses, the total net profit of Zhongguancun NEEQ companies fell to 1.541 billion yuan, a year-on-year decrease of 81.06%. After excluding three companies with great loss, the total net profit of Zhongguancun NEEQ companies in 2020 was 8.203 billion yuan, and the average net profit was 90.242 billion yuan (the regional comparison is based on the analysis of the companies except the three companies with huge losses). In contrast, the profitability of NEEQ companies in other major regions remained relatively good. In 2020, the highest total net profit of the NEEQ companies in Jiangsu is 10.711 billion yuan, and the total net profits of the NEEQ companies in Guangdong, Shanghai, and

[2] In 2020, the net profit of Zhongguancun NEEQ companies has declined more severely, mainly because three companies have suffered losses of more than 1 billion yuan under the influence of the pandemia and other factors, with a total loss of 6.662 billion yuan. Among them, CAPITAL HELICOPTER (832,494.NQ) which provide diversified general aviation services and airport services, had the highest loss in 2020 under the influence of the epidemic and the group's bankruptcy and reorganization process, reaching 2.610 billion yuan; CHINAEQUITY (833,858.NQ), one of the first independent institutions of venture capital and private equity investment in China, due to the business transformation of its holding subsidiary Hifuture Technology in 2020, the launch time of game products has been delayed, and the company has not been able to contribute revenue to the company as scheduled. The company made goodwill impairment (a total of 1.658 billion yuan) provisions for its holding subsidiaries Hifuture Technology and DKMgame, resulting in a relatively high loss of 2.474 billion yuan; HNA Cold Chain (831,900.NQ), which is committed to third-party cold chain logistics warehousing, transportation, and distribution services, has completely ceased its procurement and execution business mainly for cross-border fresh food due to the pandemia. In addition, the large provision for large amounts of bad debts and impairment of goodwill result in a loss of 1.579 billion yuan in 2020.

Zhejiang is 9.636 billion yuan, 5.169 billion yuan and 9.301 billion yuan respectively. From the point of view of average net profit, the average net profit of Zhejiang NEEQ companies is the highest, reaching 15.0265 million yuan, while those in Guangdong, Jiangsu and Shanghai are respectively 9.8231 million yuan, 12.563 million yuan and 9.69777 million yuan, which are all higher than those of Zhongguancun NEEQ companies (Data after excluding 3 companies with huge losses). In terms of growth rate, the net profit of the NEEQ companies in the five major regions increase to varying degrees in 2020. The net profit growth of the Zhongguancun NEEQ companies in 2020 is relatively small, at 0.81%. The net profit growth of Guangdong and Shanghai NEEQ companies both exceeded 50%, which are 53.47% and 71.32% respectively. The net profit growth rates of the NEEQ companies in Jiangsu and Zhejiang are 17.34% and 3.37% respectively (Fig. 5.7).

Judging from the net profit of NEEQ companies that have been operating continuously for two consecutive years from 2019 to 2020, the profitability of companies with continuous operating in the five major regions is relatively good. The net profit of Zhongguancun NEEQ companies with continuing operations in 2020 was 7.998 billion yuan, which was a steady increase from the 7.987 billion yuan in 2019. That number in Guangdong, Jiangsu, Shanghai, and Zhejiang regions was even stronger, with 9.557 billion yuan, 10.259 billion yuan, 5.063 billion yuan, and 9.212 billion yuan, respectively, whose net profit increased by more than 20% year-on-year.

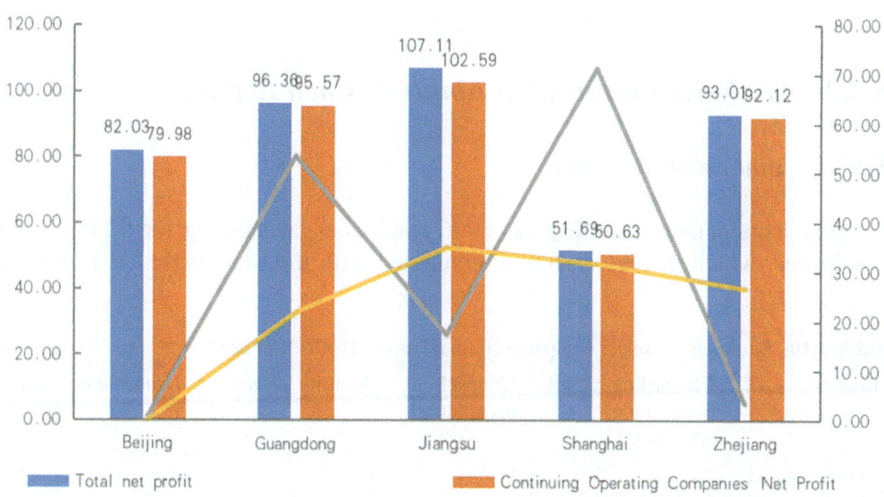

Fig. 5.7 Net profit of NEEQ Companies in major regions in 2020. *Source* Wind, compiled by ZLCA

5.3 Benchmarking Analysis of Innovation in Each Region

5.3.1 Analysis of Select Companies in Each Area

As of June 30st, 2021, the number of Select companies nationwide that have been issued is a total of 57. In terms of the number of Select counseling and filing companies nationwide, there are a total of 149 companies that have applied for counseling and filing (counseling period + acceptance), of which 25 are Zhongguancun companies (ranking first), accounting for 16.78%. There are 13 companies in Guangdong. Jiangsu, Zhejiang and Shanghai have 10 to 20 such companies. Judging from the progress of the guidance, as of June 30st, 2021, there are currently 144 enterprises in the country in the guidance period, and 5 enterprises have completed the guidance and acceptance. Judging from the application and acceptance situation of Select companies, the national guidance registration and registration accepted 137 enterprise applications, and 24 Zhongguancun enterprises (ranked first), ahead of other regions. From the NEEQ acceptance situation, as of June 30st, 2021, the NEEQ have accepted 32 Select companies, including 7 in Guangdong, 6 in Jiangsu, 3 in Zhejiang, and 1 in Zhongguancun. In terms of the number of Select companies, as of June 30st, 2021, Zhongguancun and Jiangsu are tied for the first place, both of which have 8 (Table 5.10).

5.3.2 Analysis of Innovation Ability in Each Region

5.3.2.1 Innovation Resources

In 2020, Zhongguancun NEEQ has 8996 employees, accounting for 6.21% of all employees, which increased slightly compared with the same period last year. In

Table 5.10 Situations of select companies in major areas (Unit: Number)

Region	Counseling record registration acceptance	Counseling acceptance	Quantity accepted	Issued companies
zhongguancun	24	0	1	8
guangdong	13	0	7	6
jiangsu	19	0	6	8
zhejiang	15	0	3	2
Shanghai	8	1	2	2
national	137	5	32	57

Source Wind, compiled by ZLCA

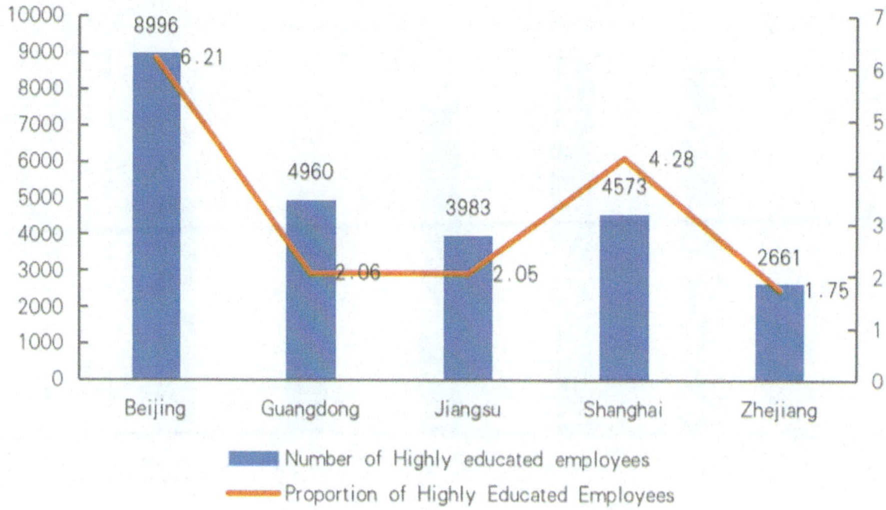

Fig. 5.8 Analysis of the number and proportion of Masters and Doctors Employees in each major region in 2020. *Source* Wind, compiled by ZLCA

terms of regional comparison, the number of master and doctor employees and their proportions in Zhongguancun ranks first (Fig. 5.8).

5.3.2.2 Innovation Force

In 2020, the R&D expenses of Zhongguancun NEEQ Companies is 7.172 billion yuan, the average R&D expenses is 9,758,400 yuan, and the average R&D intensity is 4.44%. Compared with other regions, the R&D intensity of Zhongguancun NEEQ companies is second only to Guangdong's 5.62% and Zhejiang's 4.54%. Its R&D expenses are second only to Guangdong's 7.521 billion yuan, and higher than Jiangsu's 6.475 billion yuan, Zhejiang's 4.551 billion yuan and Shanghai's 4.45 billion yuan. The average R&D expenses is 97.584 billion yuan, second only to Shanghai's 103.253 billion yuan (Fig. 5.9).

5.4 Summary

Through the analysis of the basic situation, profitability and innovation capabilities of major regions across the country, it can be seen that in 2020, in the context of the outbreak of the COVID-19 and the continued downward trend of the macroeconomy, the number of National NEEQ companies has continued to decrease, and the indicators above in the major regions are getting better under pressure.

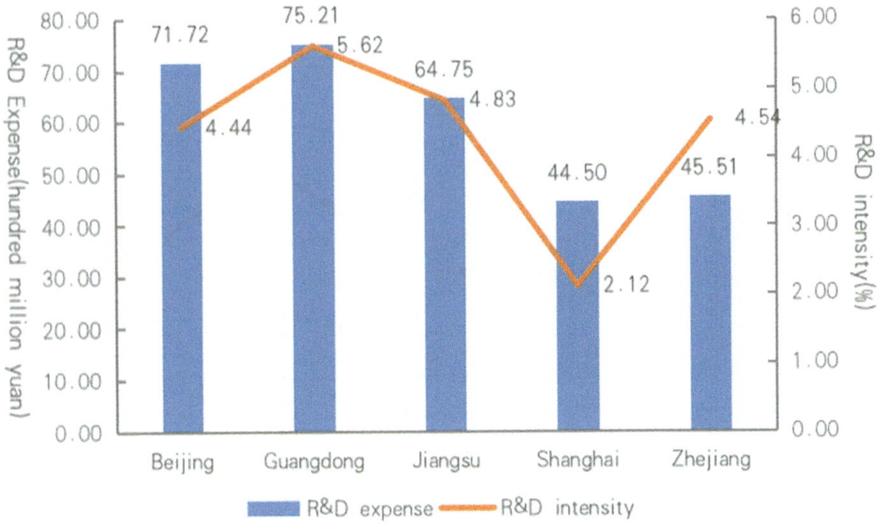

Fig. 5.9 R&D expenses and intensity of each major region in 2020. *Source* Wind, compiled by ZLCA

The total market value and total assets of Zhongguancun NEEQ companies are still leading the country while under downward pressure. In 2020, the total market value and total assets of all major regions in the country show an improvement trend. The total assets of Zhongguancun NEEQ enterprises have been ranked first in the country, and the total market value is in the forefront. This shows the good foundation and investors' confidence in Zhongguancun NEEQ companies.

In 2020, the total financing of NEEQ listed companies in the country and the above five regions improve to a certain extent compared with 2019. The financing capacity of NEEQ companies has relatively improved, but the overall financing capabilities of NEEQ companies are still at an advantage, especially absolute advantage in bond issuance. Compared with listed companies, NEEQ companies have relatively weak financing capabilities through multiple methods of direct financing. They need to cooperate with financial institutions to innovate more financial products and promote the capital operation of NEEQ companies.

In 2020, the proportion of actual taxes in revenue in each major region drops significantly, and the average actual tax burden in Zhongguancun shows a downward trend. Zhongguancun has made great efforts to reduce taxes for NEEQ companies that have been operating for two consecutive years from 2019 to 2020. Both the amount of income tax and the proportion of revenue to total profit have been significantly reduced, but the proportion of income tax to total profit is still at a relatively high level (about 5 percentage points higher than Jiangsu, which accounts for the lowest proportion), the tax reduction of Zhongguancun NEEQ Companies need to be further strengthened.

In 2020, the total number of employees, the average number of employees, and the average number of bachelors, masters and doctors' employees in all major regions decrease to varying degrees. The total number, the average number and proportion of bachelors, masters and doctors' employees in Zhongguancun NEEQ companies are higher than those in other regions, which means that they have employees with high quality.

The revenue of all regions has decreased in various degree. Compared with the others, Zhongguancun NEEQ companies have the highest revenue and lowest decrease trend.

The innovation ability of Zhongguancun NEEQ companies have been slightly worse, but the number of select companies is 8, ranking first with Guangdong. In terms of R&D intensity of Zhongguancun NEEQ companies, it is lower than that of Guangdong and Jiangsu.

Special Subject 1: Analysis of NEEQ Delisting Companies

Overview of the Number of NEEQ Companies

Since the expansion of the NEEQ in 2013, the number of companies listed on the NEEQ market has grown rapidly, and the NEEQ has ushered in explosive growth. On January 24st, 2014, there were 266 companies listed on the NEEQ at one time. The listed companies broke 10,000 for the first time in 2016 and reached their peak in 2017, with a total of 11,630 listed companies. In the process of rapid development, some companies have delisted due to transfer to A-share listings, active application for delisting, mergers and acquisitions, and failure to disclose regular reports on time. As of December 31st, 2020, there are a total of 5,172 delisted companies on the NEEQ. Among them, the number of delisted companies in 2019 is the largest, close to 2,000, and Zhongguancun will decrease by 258; in 2020, there will be a total of 903 delisted companies on the NEEQ and 115 in Zhongguancun. Compared with the reduction in the number of enterprises in 2019, the number was reduced by 54.55% and 55.42% respectively, which was a significant decrease year-on-year (Fig. A.1).

Types of NEEQ Delisting Companies

Regulations on the Delisting of NEEQ Enterprises

The "Business Rules for the National Equities Exchange and Quotations System for Small and Medium-sized Enterprises (for Trial Implementation)" that came into effect on February 8st, 2013 stipulates the following provisions regarding the delisting of NEEQ companies: If a listed company encounters one of the following circumstances, the equity exchange company shall terminate its shares Listing:

Zhongguancun Listed Companies Association, *The Growth Report of Zhongguancun NEEQ Listed Companies (2021)*, Current Chinese Economic Report Series,
https://doi.org/10.1007/978-981-19-1242-9

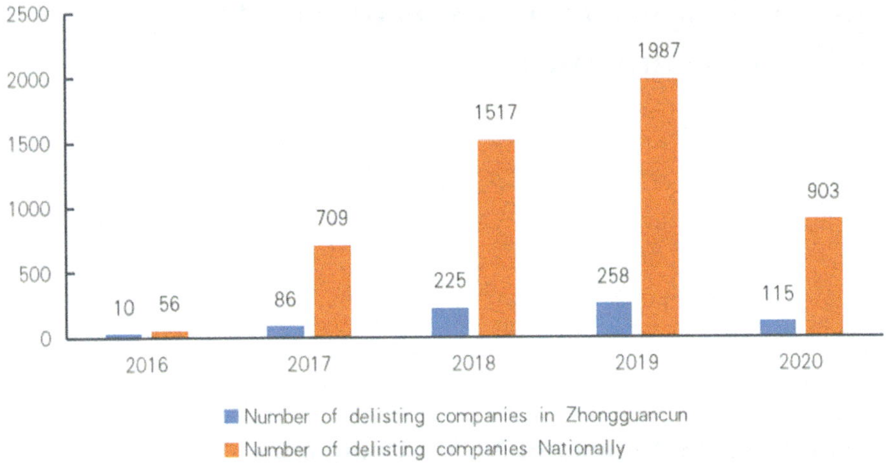

Fig. A.1 The number of delisting companies on the National and Zhongguancun NEEQ in 2016–2020. *Source* Wind, compiled by ZLCA

1. The China Securities Regulatory Commission approves its public offering and listing on the stock exchange, or the stock exchange approves the listing of its stock.
2. The application for termination of listing was approved by the National Equity Exchange System Company.
3. If the annual report or semi-annual report is not disclosed within the prescribed time limit, the annual report or semi-annual report has not been disclosed within two months from the expiration date.
4. The lead broker and the listed company terminate the continuous supervision agreement, and the listed company fails to sign the continuous supervision agreement with other lead brokers within three months from the date of stock transfer.
5. The listed company is liquidated by the liquidation group or manager and the company registration is cancelled.
6. Other circumstances stipulated by the National Equity Exchange System Company.

Types of NEEQ Delisting Companies

In summary, the delisting of the NEEQ companies can be divided into two categories, namely, the listed company actively applies for termination of listing, and the listed company is forcibly terminated by the National Equity Exchange System Corporation (hereinafter referred to as the Equity Transfer Company or NEEQ).

On January 29st, 2021, the equity exchange company issued the "Implementation Rules for the Termination of Listing of Companies Listed on the National SME Equity

Exchange System (Draft for Solicitation of Comments)" (hereinafter referred to as "Implementation Rules"), in which Article 7 of Chapter 2 stipulates the following 3 cases of voluntary termination of listing:

1. The company is dissolved. The shareholders' meeting of the listed company resolved to dissolve.
2. Company merger. The listed company is no longer qualified as an independent entity and is cancelled due to a newly established merger or merger by absorption.
3. Bottom line terms. Other applications for termination of listing as recognized by the National Equities Exchange and Quotations.

Article 16 of Chapter 3 provides for the mandatory termination of listing. Compared with the original, three new situations have been added. The details are as follows:

1. Failure to disclose periodic reports. Failure to disclose the annual report or interim report within the statutory period, or the disclosed annual report or interim report has not been reviewed and approved by the board of directors of the listed company, or more than half of the directors cannot fully guarantee the authenticity, accuracy and accuracy of the annual report or interim report disclosed by the company Completeness, or the financial report in the annual report has not been audited by an accounting firm that meets the requirements of the Securities Law, and the foregoing circumstances have not been disclosed or corrected within two months from the expiration of the statutory period.
2. Information disclosure is not credible. The financial and accounting reports of the last two years have been issued by certified public accountants with negative or inability to express opinions.
3. The net assets are negative. The audited net assets at the end of the last three fiscal years are all negative.
4. Major violations of the law. Major violations involving national security, public safety, ecological safety, production safety, and public health and safety were held accountable, resulting in the suspension of business licenses, closure orders, or cancellation of listed companies or their main subsidiaries in accordance with the law, and their suspensions in accordance with the law The main business production and operation license, or other circumstances where the legal qualification to continue production and operation is lost.
5. Fraudulent issuance, illegal information disclosure, etc. In the event of fraudulent issuance, illegal information disclosure, etc., the listed company or relevant responsible persons were sentenced to be guilty and effective by the people's court in accordance with Article 160 or Article 161 of the Criminal Law.
6. Conceal important facts or fabricate major false content. For concealing important facts or fabricating material false content in the publicly announced stock transfers and securities issuance documents, he was subject to administrative penalties by the China Securities Regulatory Commission and its dispatched agencies.

7. Fraudulent listing. He did not meet the listing conditions and defrauded the National Equity Exchange Corporation to obtain a listing approval letter and was publicly condemned.
8. The cumulative number of public condemnations reached three times. Except for the circumstances stipulated in Items 6 and 7 of this Article, the number of administrative penalties by the China Securities Regulatory Commission and its dispatched agencies or public condemnation by the national equity exchange company for different matters has reached three times in the past 24 months.
9. There are doubts about the ability to continue operations. There are matters that affect its ability to continue operations as stipulated by the accounting standards, and the main securities firm has issued a special opinion that it does not have the ability to continue operations, and after three months, the sponsoring brokerage has verified that it has issued a special opinion and believes that the situation has not been eliminated.
10. Unsound corporate governance-refer to the listing conditions. The general meeting of shareholders cannot be convened in accordance with the law, the general meeting of shareholders cannot form effective resolutions, or the listed company has lost contact channels for information disclosure, refuses to disclose material information that should be disclosed, or seriously disrupts the order of information disclosure, etc., the sponsored securities firm's corporate governance mechanism is not sound or information Disclosure of special opinions with major deficiencies, and after six months, the sponsoring securities firm has verified that the special opinions have been verified and believes that the situation has not been eliminated.
11. There is no sponsoring brokerage supervision. Cancel the continuous supervision agreement with the main brokerage firm and fail to sign the continuous supervision agreement with other main brokerage firms within three months.
12. Mandatory dissolution. Was forcibly disbanded in accordance with the law.
13. Declare bankruptcy. Was declared bankrupt by the court.
14. Bottom line terms. Other circumstances recognized by the National Equity Exchange Corporation.

The Reason and Destination of Zhongguancun Delisting Companies

From 2016 to 2020, the number of Zhongguancun NEEQ delisting companies totaled 698. Among them, 299 are active to delist,[1] accounting for 42.84% of all delisting companies, and 399 were forced to delist due to "non-disclosure of periodic reports after the suspension of listing" or other non-compliance with the listing. Table A.1

[1] Note: The adjustment of production and operation, backdoor listing, and the merger by absorption belong to active delisting; the failure to disclose periodic reports after the suspension of listing and other circumstances that are not in compliance with the listing are compulsory delisting.

Table A.1 Reasons for the delisting of Zhongguancun companies from 2016 to 2020 (Unit: Number)

Reason for termination of listing/year	2016	2017	2018	2019	2020	In total
Adjustment of production and operation	0	25	80	90	62	257
Failure to disclose periodic reports after the suspension of listing	4	9	20	58	22	113
Backdooring listing	2	10	11	9	6	38
The merger by absorption	1	2	0	0	0	3
Other circumstances that are not in compliance with the listing	3	41	114	102	25	285
In total	10	87	225	259	115	696

Source Wind, compiled by ZLCA

shows the reasons for the delisting of 696 enterprises in Zhongguancun from 2016 to 2020.

Active Delisting

It can be seen from Table A.1 that from 2016 to 2020, a total of 698 NEEQ companies in Zhongguancun were delisting. Among them, 299 are active to delist, accounting for 42.84% of all delisting enterprises in Zhongguancun. The main reasons include backdoor listing, mergers and acquisitions, and production and operation adjustments, which accounted for 5.44%, 0.43%, and 36.96% of all delisting companies, respectively. More than 30% of the enterprises applied for voluntary delisting on the grounds of production and management adjustments for the following reasons.

There Are Variables in the Listing or Merger Plan

According to the current delisting rule system, companies do not need to apply for delisting when they start preparing for an IPO, preparing for mergers and acquisitions, or major asset reorganizations. Only when the China Securities Regulatory Commission approves the public offering of shares and listing on the stock exchange or after the merger, the entity qualification is cancelled, the company is changed to a limited liability company, or the acquirer or the acquisition does not comply with the "Administrative Measures for the Acquisition of Non-listed Public Companies" Delisting. Therefore, unless the IPO has passed, there is no conflict between the IPO and the listing on the New OTC.

If a company apply for delisting when planning an IPO, it can avoid the information disclosure problems of the NEEQ during the IPO review period and the corporate dilemma caused by the inconsistent review standards of the equity exchange company and the China Securities Regulatory Commission. However, there will be uncertainty after the IPO. If the IPO review fails after delisting, the company will become an ordinary joint-stock company. How to arrange the gambling agreement signed by the company and the actual controller, and how to arrange the interests of investors will become a company's problem. Therefore, most companies currently choose a more conservative strategy, which is to delist after the company's IPO. However, some companies' listing or M&A plans involve other stakeholders, or some adjustments are needed, or there are still variables, which are not convenient for public disclosure for the time being. Therefore, the reasons are explained in a relatively vague way when delisting, to leave room for it.

There May Be Forced to Delist

Companies that have doubts about their ability to continue operations or may be forced to delist due to other reasons can actively apply for delisting and clearly disclose the reasons, or they can choose not to act and wait for forced delisting, but both practices are detrimental to the corporate image, so the company is more likely to choose to actively apply for delisting but explain the reason for the delisting in a relatively vague way.

On the other hand, according to the *Executive Rules for the Termination of Listing*, "the listed company whose shares are forcibly terminated from listing and the relevant responsible entities shall make arrangements and disclose the appeals of shareholders. The controlling shareholder and actual controller of the listed company or the listed company, and the main securities firm of the listed company can set up a special fund to compensate shareholders." Therefore, the forced delisting will increase the responsibility of the main securities firm and the controlling shareholder and actual controller of the listed company. At the same time, for companies that are at risk of forced delisting, due to information disclosure issues, the company and its chairman, general manager, board secretary, and chief financial officer are at risk of being punished by the equity exchange company. In order to solve the information disclosure problem, avoid aggravated punishment, the company can apply for voluntary delisting before being forced to delist.

Out of the Balance of the Cost and Benefit of Maintaining the Listing

Although the reform has led to the improvement of overall NEEQ market liquidity, there are still many high-quality companies whose actual financing needs cannot be met, and many companies, especially traditional companies, rarely receive investors' attention. As of December 31st, 2020, the total number of stocks traded on the Zhongguancun NEEQ trading market was 712, with a transaction volume of 272,287,500 shares, a turnover of 1.487 billion yuan, and a turnover rate of only 0.03%.

In addition, in recent years, the NEEQ market has become more stringent in supervision, which has led to an increase in the compliance costs of companies listed on the NEEQ or on-board companies. Listed companies generally have an earlier development stage and a faster development speed, but their own profitability is limited. The cost of listing on the NEEQ is relatively high. In addition, companies listed on the NEEQ need to pay management fees every year, so the high cost leads to poor profitability. Of companies choose to delist.

Passive Delisting

From 2016 to 2020, a total of 399 NEEQ companies in Zhongguancun were delisting due to "non-disclosure of periodic reports after the suspension of listing" or other circumstances that did not comply with the listing. Among them, 114 companies did not disclose regular reports, accounting for 16.33% of all delisting companies, and the remaining 285 were due to violations of the NEEQ regulations and other non-compliance with listing, accounting for 40.83% of all delisting companies.

Judging from the announcement, the reasons given by the companies that were unable to perform their information disclosure obligations on time were mostly "unable to pay audit fees", "not able to hire an audit agency", etc. The real reason why some companies could not hire an audit agency was still due to violations of funds and transactions of them. For example, He Nan Rainbow Light Netwofk Printing Co., Ltd. (834226.NQ) is due to illegal guarantees, connected transactions have not been reviewed, and the management of official regulations is not standardized, and bank accounts are frozen; Shenyang Tianzhong Electrical Alloy Co., Ltd. (832011.NQ) is due to illegal guarantees, illegal disclosures, and non-disclosures. It is not possible to hire an audit agency for important information and other activities.

Other circumstances that do not comply with the listing include: fraudulent listing; administrative penalties identified by the CSRC as a major violation of the law, or transferred to the public security organs by the CSRC in accordance with the law; three disciplinary actions against the equity exchange company in the last 36 months; corporate governance deadlock and failure convening or failing to form a valid shareholder meeting resolution for up to 12 months; the company's ability to continue operations is doubtful; there is no supervision of the sponsoring brokerage within three months; it is forced to dissolve according to law; Declared bankrupt by the court and other circumstances recognized by the equity exchange company. For example, Shanghai Ambrosia Pharmaceutical Co., Ltd. (839248.NQ) is the company's actual controller who failed to disclose illegal guarantees as required; Rongxing Guarantee (835023.NQ) is due to financing and other plans subject to the NEEQ policy restrictions (May 27st, 2016, NEEQ issued the "Notice on Matters Concerning the Listing and Financing of Financial Enterprises", stipulating that the acceptance of small loan companies, financing guarantee companies, financial leasing companies, commercial factoring companies, pawn companies, and other financial enterprises with financial attributes will be suspended until the relevant regulatory policies are clarified For listing applications, financial companies that have already been listed may not use market-making transfer methods, and apply differentiated information disclosure and regulatory requirements).

The mandatory delisting behavior highlights that the national equity exchange companies have strengthened the supervision and management of the NEEQ by increasing penalties and other methods. On the one hand, it is conducive to purifying the NEEQ market environment, shaping a rational investment philosophy, highlighting the investment value of the NEEQ market, and attracting long-term funds to enter the market. On the other hand, it is also conducive to enhancing the vitality of market entities, forming a good mechanism for survival of the fittest, further improving the function of the capital market, and helping the long-term stable and healthy development of the capital market.

In 2020, there were 115 delisting companies in Zhongguancun. Among them, the number of companies that were delisting because they did not disclose periodic reports after the suspension of listing was 22, accounting for 19.13%; the number of companies that were delisting because of other non-compliance with the listing situation was 25, accounting for 21.74%. There are 6 companies delisting due to the backdoor listing, accounting for 5.22%. 62 companies have chosen to delist due to adjustments in production and operation, accounting for 53.91% (Fig. A.2). Among them, there are 47 passively delisting companies, accounting for 41%.

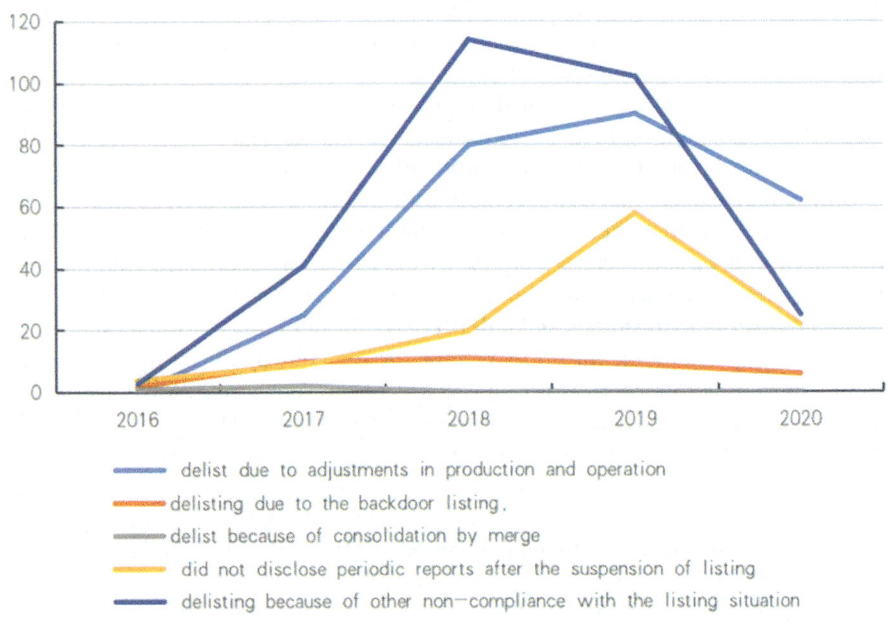

Fig. A.2 Classification of reasons for NEEQ delisting companies from 2016 to 2020. *Source* Wind, compiled by ZLCA

The NEEQ Delisting Mechanism Is Further Improved

The delisting system is the basic system of the NEEQ market. With the implementation of the comprehensive deepening of the NEEQ reform, it has initially formed a relatively benign market ecology, the market environment has undergone new changes, and listed companies have also had new demands. Improving the NEEQ termination system is an inevitable requirement for making better the quality of listed companies.

In order to improve the exit mechanism of the NEEQ market, promote the formation of a benign market entry and exit ecology, effectively protect the legitimate rights and interests of investors, and improve the quality of listed companies, in accordance with the unified deployment of China Securities Regulatory Commission, in base with "Measures for the Supervision and Administration of Non-listed Public Companies" and "Guiding Opinions on the Termination of the Listing System of the NEEQ System" (hereinafter referred to as the "Guiding Opinions") and other relevant regulations, the NEEQ formulated the "Detailed Rules for the Termination of Listing of Listed Companies in the National Small and Medium-sized Enterprise Share Transfer System" (hereinafter referred to as the "Rules for Termination of Listing"), and revised the "Guidelines for Listed Companies to Apply for Termination of Listing and Withdrawal of Termination of Listing Business" and released on May 28st, 2021.

Overall, the formulation of the "Rules for Termination of Listing" adheres to the principles of marketization and rule of law, follows the concept of combining bottom-line supervision and company autonomy, and fully summarizes the practical experience of delisting in recent years. In the early stage, the NEEQ has publicly solicited opinions on the "Rules for Termination of Listing" and based on linking up with the upper "Guiding Opinions", the rules and terms have been revised and improved. Compared with the draft for comments, the "Rules for Termination of Listing" issued further clarified the specific time points for IPO or backdoor listing companies to exempt dissenting shareholder protection measures, supplemented the relevant provisions for withdrawal of applications for delisting, and simplified the responsibilities of securities companies that handle information disclosure and related businesses in the special area are described. The revised "Rules for Termination of Listing" consists of seven chapters with 46 articles, including:

> The first is to optimize the conditions and procedures for delisting. Respect the listing company's decision to delist based on its autonomy and based on fulfilling relevant decision-making procedures and information disclosure obligations in accordance with the law, and fully protecting the legitimate rights and interests of investors, the National Equity Exchange Corporation allows listed companies to voluntarily apply for delisting. In terms of dissenting shareholders, if the protection measures are unreasonable and they refuse to correct the company that does not meet the conditions for voluntary termination of listing, it will reject its application for voluntary delisting. At the same time, the requirement of "delegating management and service" need to be implemented, and the requirement

of hiring a lawyer to issue legal opinions in the voluntary delisting is cancelled. Only the sponsoring brokerage firm needs to issue special opinions on continuous supervision to effectively reduce the burden of listed companies.

The second is to improve the circumstances and requirements for the mandatory termination of listing. Based on the current situation where the annual report or semi-annual report is not disclosed on time, and there is no continuous supervision by the sponsoring brokerage firm, four major categories and twelve types of mandatory termination of listing have been added to resolutely clear out inferior companies and improve the market's self-purification function. Specifically include: unreliable information disclosure, such as two consecutive years of financial reports issued by an accounting firm with negative opinions or inability to express opinions, more than half of the directors are not fidelity to the company's annual or semi-annual reports, etc.; loss of ability to continue operations, such as the end of three consecutive years the net assets are negative, the sponsored securities firm has issued a special opinion that does not have the ability to continue operations, and it cannot be restored within the prescribed period, is forced to dissolve in accordance with the law, and is declared bankrupt. Loss of information disclosure contact channels, etc., the sponsored bakerage firm issued a special opinion that the corporate governance mechanism is not sound or the information disclosure has major defects and cannot be restored within the prescribed time limit; there are major violations of laws and regulations, including fraudulent issuance, fraudulent listing, illegal issuance, major violations of information disclosure and major violations involving national security, public safety, ecological safety, production safety, and public health and safety.

The third is to improve investor protection measures. Investor protection is the top priority for delisting. In the process of active delisting, the listed company is required to formulate reasonable protective measures for dissenting shareholders and approved by the general meeting of shareholders, and the sponsoring broker must express clear opinions on the rationality of the protective measures for dissenting shareholders. For Select companies and Innovation and Base companies with more than 200 shareholders, a mechanism of online voting and separate voting by small and medium shareholders will be implemented. In the process of compulsory delisting, the listed companies and the sponsoring brokerages are required to fully disclose risks, actively respond to shareholders' demands, and effectively protect investors' right to know and participate. At the same time, a delisting arrangement period of ten trading days is set up to fully protect investors' exit opportunitie.

The fourth is to clearly terminate the follow-up arrangements for listing. To promote the interconnection of multi-level capital market, the National Equity Exchange Corporation encourages listed companies to go to the regional equity market for share registration and custody or transfer after delisting. At the same time, for terminated companies with more than 200 shareholders, considering their public company attributes, and in accordance with the requirements of the "Guiding Opinions", the NEEQ has set up a service area for non-public electronic transfer of delisting securities (hereinafter referred to as the "delisting securities service area"). It provides equity exchange and information disclosure services. The delisting securities service zone adopts a non-disclosure agreement transfer method in accordance with the law, implements investor suitability management and T + 5 mechanism, and the borkerage company handles the information disclosure and related business of 200 people who terminate the listed company in the zone on behalf of investors, to meet the basic requirements of investors transfer needs and the company's information disclosure requirements, while preventing risk transmission.

Special Subject 2: Exploration of the Development Path of the Capital Market of Zhongguancun NEEQ Companies

——Research on Issues Related to SPAC Listing

As of the end of June 2021, there are 31 Zhongguancun NEEQ companies that have been transferred to the A-share listing. Although the NEEQ, like listed companies, are both public companies, they are still non-listed companies. For companies, seeking further capital market development through listing is of great significance to companies in terms of financing, improving governance, and improving corporate reputation. At present, the international and domestic capital markets are developing rapidly, and there are many ways for companies to launch, such as domestic and overseas IPOs, backdoor listings, and SPAC listings. Since 2020, the number of global companies listed on SPAC has exploded. SPAC, as an innovative way of listing in the U.S. capital market, has been increasingly recognized by companies and investors. On November 19st, 2020, Orisun Acquisition Corp., a special purpose acquisition company (hereinafter referred to as "SPAC"), and Beijing-based enterprise Youke Workshop jointly announced the completion of the merger. Youke Workshop officially landed on the U.S. stock market by way of SPAC, becoming the "first share of joint office". There are many companies planning to be listed on the NEEQ. As a special way of listing, SPAC listing has its inherent advantages and disadvantages. For some NEEQ companies, SPAC listing is an important way for companies to enter the capital market. Based on this, this article conducts an in-depth analysis of the way of listing on SPAC, and would like to provide a reference for companies to be listed on the NEEQ through the way of SPAC listing.

Introduction to SPAC

Basic Information of SPAC

Zhongguancun Listed Companies Association, *The Growth Report of Zhongguancun NEEQ Listed Companies (2021)*, Current Chinese Economic Report Series,
https://doi.org/10.1007/978-981-19-1242-9

SPAC is the abbreviation for "Special Purpose Acquisition Company", which is called a derivative form of the "Blank Check Company" in the United States. The company was established without any commercial purpose or promise, but only for some future undefined object to raise funds. SPAC is made up of the original promoters, the purpose is to raise funds through IPO, and then use it to buy existing business. The funds raised in the SPAC's IPO must be deposited in an interest-bearing trust account until a suitable target company is determined. Then, the funds can only be used to fund the acquisition of the target company. SPAC itself needs to determine the target and complete the acquisition within a limited time, usually between 18 and 24 months after the IPO. If SPAC cannot complete the acquisition before the applicable deadline, the funds raised in the IPO will be returned to investors with interest on the funds.

Development of SPAC Market

SPAC can only be traded on the over-the-counter market and the US stock exchange. In 2008, the subprime mortgage crisis swept the world. To activate the financial market, the SPAC listing system was adjusted. NASDAQ and the New York Stock Exchange specially formulated listing requirements for SPAC. In addition to SPAC being very mature in the US market, London, England was the European center of SPAC around 2000. In 2009, South Korea became the first country in Asia to introduce SPAC listings.

Table B.1 Statistics of Global SPAC listings since 2009

Time (year)	Amount of IPO	Total financing (million dollars)	Average financing scale (million dollars)
2021.5.31	308	89,720.8	291.3
2020	248	83,334.7	352.6
2019	59	13,600.3	230.5
2018	46	10,751.9	233.7
2017	34	10,048.5	295.5
2016	13	3,499.2	269.2
2015	20	3,902.4	195.1
2014	12	1,749.8	145.8
2013	10	1,455.3	145.5
2012	9	490.5	54.5
2011	15	1,081.5	72.1
2010	7	502.6	71.8
2009	1	36.0	36.0
Total	726	210,917.00	/

In 2020, the SPAC listing method ushered in an explosive year. There is a total of 248 IPOs in the United States through the SPAC method. According to statistics from the SPAC insider website, as of May 31st, 2021, the number of global SPAC companies IPOs has reached 308, with an average corporate financing amount of US$291 million. The number of SPAC listings accounted for 39.44% of the historical total, exceeding the number of SPAC listings 248 in 2020 (Table B.1).

With the explosive growth of SPAC, many companies or investment institutions regard SPACs as an alternative way of listing new shares. Asian companies or investors have also joined the ranks of investing in SPAC and backdoor listings. Recently, it has been reported that the Hong Kong Stock Exchange is studying the introduction of SPAC related mechanisms and has begun to ask some brokers for their opinions. In addition, Singapore Exchange Chief Executive Luo Wencai also said that if the industry gains support, SGX will introduce the SPAC listing mechanism commonly known as "Blank Check Company" as soon as this year.

SPAC Operation Steps

The work of SPAC involves multiple steps, which can be divided into two stages: IPO transaction and M&A transaction.

First, it is usually initiated by three or more financial practitioners with PE (or mergers and acquisitions) experience and experts in specific industries to form a blank cheque company and purchase all the shares. The preparation time is about 2 to 4 months. The raised funds will be deposited in the escrow account and invested in government bonds, and will be released to pay the cash consideration required for the SPAC M&A transaction when the M&A transaction is completed, It will also specify the industry, region and IPO date of the target merger company in the prospectus. After the initial public offering, SPAC will go public and become a listed company. When trading securities, the initiator of the shell company is responsible for finding the target company for the merger, and due to the provisions of the listing rules, SPAC needs to complete such merger transactions within a limited time.

Secondly, when a suitable acquisition target is found, the terms of the acquisition will be negotiated, and a letter of intent (LOI, Letter of Intent) will be signed. The acquisition target should be announced, and a vote should be held among shareholders to approve or reject the commercial acquisition proposal. If the acquisition transaction is not approved in the end, shareholders will need to look for a new target, but the overall time limit stipulates that the acquisition transaction should be completed within 24 months, otherwise it will be delisting and liquidated, and the funds in the trust account will be returned to the shareholders. Each share will recover a portion of the IPO proceeds previously deposited.

SPAC Listing Process

The first step is to choose an investment bank as the organizer and share alloter of the entire SPAC transaction.

In the SPAC financing process, the priority of the investment bank is to help establish a cash shell company that meets the SEC listing requirements, and then use this shell company to complete the IPO financing and refinancing after acquiring the project company (the entity company, also known as the target company) successfully.

The second step is to set up a shell company.

Different from backdoor listing and buying shell listing, the shell company established by SPAC has clean shell resources, no historical liabilities, and related legal issues.

The third step is to issue common stocks and options to market investors in the form of trust.

The SPAC company completed an IPO within six months of its establishment and raised funds by issuing equity units. Under normal circumstances, an equity unit of SPAC consists of one common stock and several warrants.

The fourth step is to find and complete the merger and acquisition within a limited period.

Since some of the sponsors who initiated the SPAC are senior experts in a certain industry field, in the process of SPAC mergers and acquisitions, the sponsors and participants of the SPAC have clarified the areas of the merger target. Therefore, for SPAC promoters, they only need to find a target company that meets their expectations to merge with the SPAC within 24 months of listing.

In the fifth step, the stocks of the combined company can be listed and traded.

Before the 2008 subprime mortgage crisis, SPAC had no actual business and could only be listed and traded on the American OTCBB market and AMEX. Only after the merger with the industrial company and the transfer requirements are met, the merged company can be transferred to Nasdaq for listing and trading.

The Advantages, Disadvantages and Applicability of SPAC for Domestic Enterprises

Advantages and Disadvantages of SPAC Listing

The Advantages of SPAC Listing

First, the success rate of listing is high. SPAC first goes public and then acquires the target company. The transaction of acquiring the target company only requires mutual consent. There are no other reasons for the failure of the issuance, so the success rate of listing is high.

The second is low cost and short time. Generally speaking, if the preparations are properly arranged, the SPAC transaction process can be completed within six months.

Third, the financing methods are diverse and the amount is determined. In addition to raising funds from the public and institutional investors at the time of listing, SPACs can also raise funds by obtaining matching financing (PIPE) from mature hedge funds. Since both are determined through privately negotiated mergers and acquisitions between the parties to the agreement, the valuation has stronger certainty.

Fourth, some companies that cannot be listed in the traditional way, such as unprofitable companies, can be listed under the SPAC method. According to the rules of the US Securities Law, only past financial statements can be disclosed in a traditional IPO, but SPACs can market the fast-growing but unprofitable companies to the public and institutional investors by making business prospects for the companies that want to merge.

Fifth, the risk of SPAC is relatively low. If public investors are dissatisfied with the subject of the SPAC acquisition, they can exercise the redemption right to recover the principal and interest. If the target of the merger is high-quality, the stock price after the merger may rise rapidly, which will bring excess returns to investors.

The Advantages of SPAC Listing Methods Over Traditional IPOs

First, the time period is short, and it takes less than half of the IPO under the same conditions.

Second, the cost is low, and there is no need to pay underwriting fees, which account for most of the IPO expenses.

Third, there is no issuance failure due to market reasons, and the certainty of listing is 100%.

Fourth, the financing amount is determined, and the target company's valuation and pricing are fixed in advance.

Fifth, SPAC is highly dependent on managers and has a stronger incentive system for managers.

Sixth, the pricing method is different. The management team of SPAC will provide a fixed purchase price to the acquisition target.

Seventh, the cycle of issuance and the degree of cumbersomeness are different. SPAC has no substantive business to operate, and the information that needs to be disclosed is limited. Its process is more convenient than traditional IPOs and can be completed within eight weeks. However, SPAC needs to disclose the details of the acquisition target within four trading days after the completion of the acquisition. The degree of disclosure is basically the same as that of a traditional IPO.

The Risk of SPAC Listing

One is that the supervision is different from traditional IPOs. In the stage before the completion of the SPAC, the acquisition of the target company by the SPAC is a market behavior, which is different from the IPO which will be subject to strict review and supervision by the regulatory authorities. However, after the completion of the SPAC, the target company becomes a listed company, and the supervision will be the same as that of the IPO listed company.

The second is to dilute the owner's equity of the target enterprise. The form of SPAC is destined that the promoter will own many shares of the target company, which will dilute the equity of start-up investors and external investors. If the sponsor can bring substantial help to the company, it will be beneficial to the company's development, but not necessarily vice versa.

Third, for investors, the so-called guarantee for investing in SPAC is limited to before the completion of the acquisition. Once the acquisition is completed and the SPAC disintegrates, the listed company will be no different from other listed companies and have the same investment risks.

Fourth, SPAC is not conducive to maximizing the issuer's valuation. The SPAC transaction model determines that the final transaction price of the acquired company is negotiated between the two parties, and the valuation of the acquired company may be lower than that of the IPO.

The Screening Direction of SPAC Listing Target Companies

SPAC can meet the listing needs of three types of companies. First, in the current situation of unstable Sino-US relations, it is difficult for some start-up companies to list on the domestic STAR Market or ChiNext Board in the short term. Then SPAC provides overseas listings for such companies. Another option is for companies that have gambling agreements or investors seeking ways to withdraw. SPAC listing can meet the needs of companies to go public quickly; and third, it is suitable for technology-based companies that have not yet made a profit. At present, the national multi-level capital market is deepening reforms, but currently only STAR Market allows unprofitable companies to go public for financing, and STAR Market has relatively high requirements for companies to be listed.

Regarding the specific requirements of SPAC target companies, according to experts and research conditions, SPAC domestic target companies mainly need to meet industry, financial, valuation, equity structure and other conditions.

From the industry perspective, listing through SPAC is applicable to a variety of industries, but emerging industries use this method to list more. From the perspective of investor preferences, the Internet, healthcare, new energy, online education of the new economy, and new energy vehicles that have attracted the attention of American investors in recent years are more favored by investors. At present, according to incomplete statistics, China has 4 financial services, 3 pharmaceuticals, 1 Manufacturing, 1 service, 1 entertainment, and 1 leasing and commercial service companies listed in the United States in the form of SPACs (Table B.2). In addition, from the distribution of SPAC M&A target industries in 2020, the TMT industry accounts for the largest proportion, and the life, health and consumer industries also account for a large share. In addition, it also includes traditional energy, finance, real estate, landed property and other industries.

From the point of view of financial, according to the research of Zhongtai International, it is preliminarily determined that the target company needs to meet the following financial standards: (1) Small or medium-sized enterprises with high growth; (2) Established for more than 3 years and owning 3 complete fiscal years; (3) Financial norms, no legal and credit issues; (4) The annual revenue scale exceeds 100 million yuan (RMB) or more; (5) The annual net profit exceeds 10 million yuan (RMB) or more (except for potential companies with good growth potential); (6) Enterprises that cannot be determined to complete the domestic main board IPO, prepare to be listed on the NEEQ or withdraw from the NEEQ.

From the perspective of valuation, take the Hong Kong Midland Corporation (name to be confirmed), the initiator of the SPAC, as an example. The preferred value is more than US$300 million and the target company has already been invested by well-known international investment institutions. First, companies with less than US$300 million will be positioned as small and micro enterprises in the United States, and large or well-known investment institutions rarely invest in small and micro enterprises, which will affect the market outlook performance of the merged

Table 2 List of SPAC listings of some Chinese companies

Rank	Company	Time	Place	Industry
1	Original agritech limited	2005-11	Nasdaq	Pharmaceutical
2	Tianjin Yucheng Technologies Limited	2007-3-14	Nasdaq	Financial Services
3	China umbilical cord blood bank corporation group	2009-7	New York Stock Exchange	Pharmaceutical
4	Borqs technologies inc	2015-10-15	Nasdaq	Financial Services
5	Wins finance	2015-10-28	Nasdaq	Financial Services
6	China lending corporation	2016-7-7	Nasdaq	Financial Services
7	KXIN.US	2019-5-14	Nasdaq	Manufacturing
8	United family healthcare	2019-7	New York Stock Exchange	Pharmaceutical
9	Meten EdtechX	2020-4-1	Nasdaq	Education
10	Scienjoy	2020-5-7	Nasdaq	Entertainment
11	UCOMMUNE	2020-11-24	Nasdaq	Leasing and Business services

object and future continued financing to a certain extent ability; the second is the valuation of shares when a well-known investment institution invests in the target company, which can provide reference merger consideration for SPAC mergers, and SPAC investors are more likely to accept the merger consideration。

From the perspective of corporate equity structure, domestic companies need to build a red-chip structure. Currently, domestic companies listed on SPAC are all red-chip companies.

In addition, the sponsors of SPAC value the professional background of the target company's management team and shareholders. Companies with greater growth potential, already profitable, abundant cash flow, and clear shareholding structure are obviously more favored.

Types of Enterprises Applicable to SPAC Listing

Listing through SPAC is applicable to a variety of industries. At present, many emerging industries use this method to go public, but in fact, whether it is traditional or emerging industries, light assets or heavy assets, SPAC can be used. From the perspective of investor preferences, the internet, healthcare, education, gaming, new energy, and other industries in the new economy are more favored by investors. Among them, companies with greater growth potential, already profitable, abundant cash flow, and clear shareholding structure have more obvious advantages.

In general, SPAC is more suitable for start-ups in the new economy industry. Once the company is already large, the shell company needs to raise more funds, and a good merger opportunity can also be found in the SPAC. Based on previous SPAC successful cases and expert opinions from financial institutions, the following types of companies are recommended to consider SPAC listing methods:

(1) Suitable for enterprises with financing needs. According to the relevant regulations of the US SEC, the minimum amount of SPAC initiated is 50 million U.S. dollars, so the capital obtained by the company through the SPAC listing will not be less than 50 million U.S. dollars. According to statistics, as of 2021, the average financing amount of 252 SPAC listed companies has reached 319 million US dollars.

(2) Suitable for companies that have gambling agreements or investors seeking exit methods. The listing of SPAC is deterministic. For companies that have signed a listing and gambling agreement or investors are eager to withdraw, SPAC can be used as an effective means.

(3) Suitable for companies that have not yet made a profit. At present, the domestic capital market only allows unprofitable companies to conduct IPOs on the Science and Technology Innovation Board, and it is difficult for many unprofitable companies represented by biomedicine to list and raise funds in the domestic capital market.

(4) VIE structure enterprise. At present, for domestic enterprises to enter the capital market through SPAC, it is usually necessary to build a VIE structure.

Suggestions for the SPAC Listing

There are many high-tech, high-growth enterprises in Beijing. Listing financing is an important way for companies to maintain rapid development. However, it is difficult for some start-up companies to list on the domestic STAR Market or ChiNext Board in the short term. Although the NEEQ Select has landed, market liquidity still needs to be improved. SPAC, as a listing method different from traditional IPOs, can provide high-quality companies in Beijing with a path for overseas listing.

The first is to study and analyze domestic SPAC listing issues and paths. At present, SPACs are relatively mature in the US capital market, and most companies choose SPACs to be listed as market behaviors. In 2020, nearly 50% of enterprises successfully listed through SPAC, and SPAC listing is increasingly accepted by the market. It is recommended to strengthen the research on the related issues of domestic enterprises' SPAC listing, understand the factors that affect enterprises' listing through SPAC and the key and difficult issues encountered in the listing process in detail, and explore the SPAC listing model and path that meet the characteristics of Beijing enterprises.

Second, it is recommended that SPAC be continuously evaluated. It is recommended that regulatory authorities, Shanghai and Shenzhen stock exchanges, and national equity transfer companies study the regulatory and risk issues of SPAC listings, assess whether SPAC listings can be piloted and promoted in the domestic capital market, and explore the feasibility and path of NEEQ companies listing through SPACs.

The third is to carry out SPAC special training sessions. Organize investment institutions, brokerages, clubs, law firms and other financial institutions that have SPAC operation experience to carry out SPAC business, and conduct special training sessions for companies intending to list overseas to help companies understand the advantages and disadvantages of the SPAC listing model and related issues problem.

The fourth is to carry out enterprise surveys and visits in-depth. For companies in Beijing that are interested in listing through SPAC, conduct research and visits to key companies, resource docking, and problem coordination, and help companies that are willing to go public through SPAC financing.

The fifth is to increase financial support for SPAC listed companies. Enterprise's SPAC listing has the attributes of mergers and acquisitions and listing. In view of the situation of companies landing overseas capital markets through SPAC, it is recommended that SPAC listing be included in the relevant subsidy system for corporate listing and mergers and acquisitions so that SPAC listed companies can enjoy relevant financial rewards in Beijing and various districts.

The manufacturer's authorised representative in the EU is Springer Nature Customer Service Centre GmbH, Europaplatz 3, 69115 Heidelberg, Germany. If you have any concerns regarding our products, please contact ProductSafety@springernature.com

Printed and bound by CPI Group (UK) Ltd, Croydon, CR0 4YY

30/09/2026

02225259-0010